Money

Money
Its Origin, Development and Modern Use

by
Carl H. Moore
and
Alvin E. Russell

McFarland & Company, Inc., Publishers
Jefferson, North Carolina, and London

Library of Congress Cataloguing-in-Publication Data

Moore, Carl H., 1916–
 Money: its origin, development, and modern use.

 Bibliography: p. 157.
 Includes index.
 1. Money—History.   2. Money—United States—
History.   I. Russell, Alvin E.   II. Title.
HG231.M63   1987   332.4'9   87-42515

ISBN 0-89950-272-5 (acid-free natural paper) ∞

Printed in the United States of America

McFarland   Box 611   Jefferson NC 28640

Dedicated
to the memory
of Cindy

Acknowledgments

Many people have assisted the authors in preparing this material. Their wives, Beatrice Russell and Sue Moore, have read the manuscript for continuity. Constructive comments were offered by John Russell, Mr. Russell's son and by Susan Moore, Dr. Moore's daughter. Typing of the early manuscript was done by Beverly Hollje and the final copy by Kathi Glidewell. Members of the staff of the Federal Reserve banks of Dallas, Atlanta, New York and Richmond contributed ideas and information. H.T. Krisak, superintendent, Management Services Division, Department of the Treasury, Bureau of Engraving and Printing and James A. Parker, assistant to the director, Office of the Director of the Mint, were extremely helpful in providing facts and photographs. In addition, Paul D. Aschbacher, president of InterFirst Bank of Alamo Heights and C. J. Krause, senior vice president of Frost National Bank served as consultants on information relating to commercial banks. Cooperation of the U.S. Secret Service and *Coin World* also is acknowledged.

Preface

Money has been the subject of many articles and books. Some have written about its history; others have concentrated on its uses and still others on its economic effects. There are even books about the laws concerning money. The purpose of this book is to put in one place the interesting and unusual facts and customs surrounding money as well as much of its history and use.

Money is not easy to understand. Even the experts often disagree about its impact on society, and its use in making our economy work efficiently. But this book is an attempt to put in layman's language the vast information about this item that we carry in our pocket, in our checkbook, store in a piggy bank and even go to war over. It will include a brief history of money, particularly in the United States, with significant dates, facts, and highlights; how our money is made and stored; how it is issued and retired from circulation and the meaning of money in its broadest sense—the money supply.

Interesting laws about our money including those dealing with counterfeiting, legal tender and the rights of loser and finder when money is lost will be discussed. Scattered throughout the book the reader will find humorous stories about money and the story behind some of its well-known expressions.

The material assembled, including thoughts and opinions of well-known authors and other famous men, should be of considerable assistance to anyone preparing a report, an essay, or a talk on the subject of money.

Table of Contents

Chapter One
Money's Precursors

Barter Systems

A farmer in the Southwest dropped his billfold while feeding his cattle and did not miss it until he returned to the house.

"There were $600 in that billfold," he exclaimed to his wife. Back to the feed lot he went and after eyeballing each steer he pointed his finger at one and said, "You ate my billfold!" Needing some meat for the table anyway he promptly butchered the suspicious animal and sure enough, in the stomach of that steer was his billfold.

It was a mess. But undaunted, he wrapped it all in paper and placed it in a box. Then, on advice of his local banker, he shipped it off to the United States Treasury with a statement of what had happened. Experts at the Treasury carefully (and holding their noses) examined the contents of the box and positively identified $473 of the farmer's $600 and sent him a check for that amount.

Unusual? Yes. But many times the people at the Treasury are able to identify mutilated money and save people a loss. Unfortunately, there is no way to reimburse people for money that has been totally destroyed.

Money and its relation to people are the source of many stories and myths. The admonition of St. Paul to his friend Timothy that "The love of money is the root of all evil" is often misquoted as "Money is the root of all evil." Benjamin Franklin said "Money is a good servant but a poor master." But the source of the old saying that a fool and his money are soon parted is lost in antiquity.

There is much more to money than old sayings and unusual incidents. Money—a term that includes currency and coin—has a long history and is an integral part of any nation's economy. The evolution of money in its various forms is a fascinating story.

Let us go back in history to the time when man needed to "trade" with his neighbor. Certainly the cave man had no need for money as he was dependent upon his own skills as a hunter and fisherman to provide his basic needs of food, clothing and shelter. At some point, he may have traded an extra fish for the skin of an animal if he was on speaking terms with the family in the next cave.

Trading—or barter, as we would call it today—may very well have started when one man discovered that he was a better fisherman than he was a hunter, while his neighbor was more skillful with the arrow or club or whatever he used to kill wild animals. In any event, it soon became easier to trade rather than try to do everything himself. Today's barter has become more of a tax evasion gimmick than a necessity for efficient trading of goods.

As man became more skilled in trading and perhaps on more congenial terms with his neighbors, he wanted a way of storing the "values" he had gained. He did not always want another animal skin at the time he had an extra fish, but he might later. So certain items became accepted as means of holding and exchanging values. A person would receive an item that would be accepted by others in exchange for a variety of things. Thus, if he wanted a new club, he did not have to find someone who wanted his extra fish but he could use the acceptable item in exchange for his fish and then go to the man who had an extra club.

Commodity Money

Out of this experience came "commodity money." The use of commodities in trading has a varied, interesting and sometimes unbelievable history. In theory, a commodity to be accepted as "money" needs to be known to many people and has to have some recognizable value: furs would have little use as money in the tropical islands. Yet in North America and much of Europe they had value as a consumer good and thus could be used as well in barter transactions. In theory, a commodity money should also be storable and not too difficult to transport. But in many, if not most primitive societies, this was of minimal concern. The commodities used were for the most part consumer goods and the distances traveled were limited.

No doubt the use of commodity money began in the family as one member offered to give an item to another in exchange for a service or another consumer good. Even in today's modern society, members of a family often make use of commodities as they exchange a tool or a service for another item. Who hasn't watched children offer to trade a toy or a rock or a frog for a ball or a marble? Or what parent hasn't told a child, "Keep your room clean for a week and we will go to the circus"—trading a service for a pleasure.

The use of commodity money is a story in itself. And we will not dwell on the subject except to see the way in which groups of people made use of something other than money as we know it today in carrying out trade. In Paul Einzig's book, *Primitive Money,* he tells of dozens of different commodities used as money. For example, in New Guinea a variety of shells are used, the cowrie *(Cypraea moneta)* being the most common. This richly colored and naturally polished shell was highly valued and early explorers found that efforts to trade with trinkets, tobacco and other items, usually valued by primitive tribes, were useless. But when they brought cowrie shells, they were welcomed as traders.

The cowrie shell also has been used by some African tribes. In addition to its value as a means of trade, the cowrie shell derived part of its value from the frequent use as ornaments and charms to ward off evil spirits. The cowrie shell was one of the most widely used shells for primitive money. In some remote islands the "harvest" or importation of shells was controlled by the "chiefs" or other ruler and thus their value was maintained. The Maldive Islands off the southern tip of India for centuries have been one of the principal sources of the cowrie. This unique shell has been, and in some localities still is, used as "money" throughout a wide area of southern Asia, the Pacific Islands and parts of the Middle East and Africa.

Cattle are one of the best known commodities used for money. In many primitive areas cattle have been the common means of measuring value and of evaluating a trade of goods or services. Cattle have been and still are, to some extent, the measure of a man's "worth" in many sections of Africa. They became so important in some tribes that even sick or diseased cattle would not be disposed of but kept for trading purposes. Also, because the number of cattle measured a man's status in the community they were accumulated far beyond the ability of the available pasture to support them. Quality of the cattle declined and at some point it became necessary to move to another area or in some cases to take over another tribe's pasture, killing off the existing cattle and people.

Negley Farson in *Behind God's Back* states that while serving as an agricultural expert in Nakuru, Kenya, he attempted to encourage the natives not to keep their old and diseased cattle. Finally, one of the natives told him, "Here are two pound notes; one old and wrinkled and one new. But they are each worth a pound, aren't they? Well, it's the same way with cows. They are both cows." You may question his respect for quality but if you are using cows as a medium of exchange, he makes sense.

Cattle are the principal means of exchange among the Goajira Indians of Colombia in South America. According to Einzig this "commodity money" is relatively recent as cattle were not introduced to the area until the time of the Spanish Conquistadores in the sixteenth century. As in Africa, the need for continually expanding pastures to accommodate the herds of cattle was the cause of many tribal wars. Julian Weston estimated that just prior to World War II, the number of cattle owned by the Goajira Indians exceeded 100,000.

As with other groups using cattle for money, it was almost impossible to get married without a sufficient number of cattle to buy a bride. The daughter of a poor man would require fewer cattle than the daughter of a rich man. So

An example of stone money used on the island of Yap, with some stones being several feet in diameter. The hole in the middle is for a pole so that two people can carry it. (Photo courtesy of *Coin World*.)

the price of a bride might vary from two or three head to 200 head of cattle. The quality of the cattle is never mentioned.

Salt is another commodity that has had wide usage as money, probably most extensively in Ethiopia. There it served as a medium of exchange as recently as 1935 when the Italians invaded the country. Even today, it is the most accepted money in some remote areas. The usual form as used in Ethiopia was in bars of rock salt about ten to twelve inches long and one-and-a-half inches thick, and the bars were referred to as "amoles." Contrary to our usual image of salt these bars usually were black, having acquired the color from much handling. According to Captain Alexander Hamilton in his book *A New Account of the East Indies*, Ethiopians are experts in dividing these bars as they pay for goods. They skillfully pinch off the required amount and pass it to the seller. In the interior of New Guinea salt also was used as a medium of exchange.

On the Pacific island of Alor, the common commodity for money is a drum. Cora Du Bois in her book, *The People of Alor,* states that she could hardly conduct her research on the psychology of the area for all the talk about drums. These metal drums were used as a medium of exchange only if they were damaged. Gongs also played a part in the commodity money of the island. Du Bois reported that pigs were high in value but were used mostly for ceremonial celebrations at which the pig was the main course.

Would you believe that a stone twice the size of a grown man could serve as commodity money? It's true. On the Pacific island of Yap, stones were the principal measure of value until the advent of World War II. Even today, Yapees place large stones in front of their houses to indicate wealth. These stones had to be imported from the islands of Guam and Pelew; they were not available on the island of Yap. This accounts for part of their value—scarcity. The stones are in the shape of a disk with a hole in the center through which a pole can be inserted to aid in transporting them. Smaller stones are freely used in conducting transactions on the island. Many of the larger stones carry inscriptions giving the time and place they were quarried, names of owners and other pertinent information. Some are estimated to be 200 or more years old.

Here's an interesting one for all economists: on Rossel Island, off the coast of New Guinea, is one of the most complicated payment systems ever devised by man. There are two kinds of money on the island, one called "ndap" and the other called "nko"; ndap is individual pieces of the *Spondylus* shell; nko is made up of sets of ten shell disks made from a giant clam. There are twenty-two different values of ndap and sixteen different values of nko. Only the lower units of ndap circulate but all units of nko circulate freely. Just to confuse you further, ndap is regarded as man's money but nko is women's money. Now try this on your pocket calculator. If you borrow a unit called "4" you repay with a unit called "5" or "6," or maybe "7" or "8," depending on how long you keep the unit. If you borrow in a higher unit, you must repay with the same unit but the interest must be repaid with the smaller units.

Although shells of various kinds may have been the most widely used item for commodity money, they were not commodity money in the strictest sense since they had limited consumer value. But they served the purpose of facilitating transactions and so we are including them in this discussion.

Wampum

We have already talked about the cowrie, that unique, colorful shell, but probably the best known shell to Americans is wampum, also known as wampumpeag, or peag. Wampum consisted of two kinds of beads, one white and the other black. The white ones were made from the end of a periwinkle shell

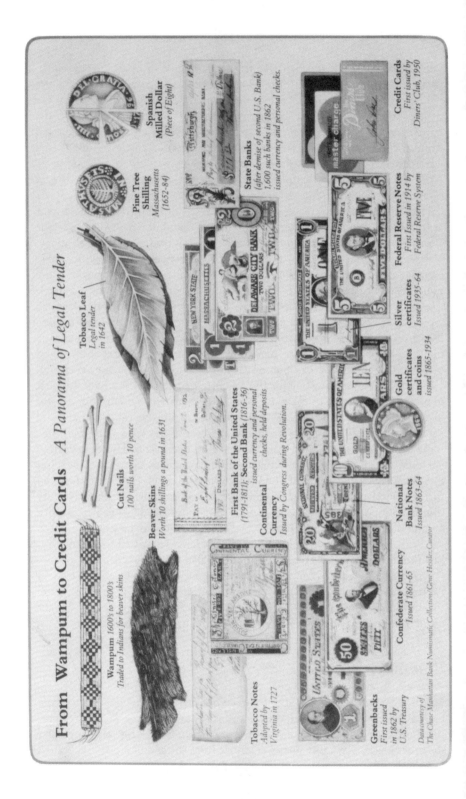

From Wampum to Credit Cards   A Panorama of Legal Tender

Wampum 1600's to 1800's
Traded to Indians for beaver skins

Tobacco Notes
*Adopted by
Virginia in 1727*

Greenbacks
*First issued
in 1862 by
U.S. Treasury*

Beaver Skins
Worth 10 shillings a pound in 1631

Cut Nails
100 nails worth 10 pence

**Continental
Currency**
Issued by Congress during Revolution.

First Bank of the United States
*(1791-1811); Second Bank (1816-36)
issued currency and personal
checks, held deposits*

Confederate Currency
Issued 1861-65

Tobacco Leaf
*Legal tender
in 1642*

**Pine Tree
Shilling**
*Massachusetts
(1652-84)*

**Spanish
Milled Dollar**
(Piece of Eight)

State Banks
*(after demise of second U.S. Bank)
1,600 such banks in 1862
issued currency and personal checks.*

**National
Bank Notes**
Issued 1863-64

**Gold
certificates
and coins**
issued 1865-1934

**Silver
certificates**
Issued 1935-64

Federal Reserve Notes
*First Issued in 1914 by
Federal Reserve System*

Credit Cards
*First issued by
Diners Club, 1950*

*Data courtesy of
The Chase Manhattan Bank Numismatic Collection/Gene Hessler, Curator*

and the black ones from the black part of a clam shell. The word wampum literally means "string of white shell beads." Making wampum required long hours and much skill. Lindstrom reports that a day's output amounted to only a few pence a day. The beads or parts of the shells were rubbed down and polished. Then they were strung on strings or belts, or made into jewelry of various kinds. Generally, one black bead was worth two white beads; a fathom, or belt of wampum, consisted of 360 beads.

One of the reasons wampum was used as money was that it was largely imperishable, easily divided and not very bulky. It was accepted in payment for both large and small items and for some time it was a general rule in the North American colonies that unless some other means was specified, it was assumed that it would be in wampum. Wampum was used almost exclusively as a medium of exchange by the Indians of Northeastern United States and by the colonists both in transactions with the Indians and between themselves. A shortage of European money made it much more convenient to use wampum.

Wampum was made "legal tender" in Massachusetts for 12d (pennies). However, it was used for all transactions and was the prevailing medium of exchange. One of the limitations of wampum, and the factor that led eventually to the use of other items, was that it was not accepted for export and would not satisfy foreign debts. While the demand for beaver skins in Europe remained strong, wampum was widely used as it was readily exchanged for beaver skins. But when the demand for beaver skin declined, wampum lost some of its value. Also, it wasn't long before the white man found ways of counterfeiting wampum and that destroyed much of its value.

On the West Coast of the United States a bead from detalium was more common. This was not as standard as wampum and the value varied with the color and size of the beads.

Many commodity monies were items of intrinsic value such as cattle, salt, and rice. Others such as shells and beads had little if any intrinsic value except as ornaments. Even pieces of metal that could have had intrinsic value often were not used except as money. Primitive axes have apparently been used as money and yet they were of such size as to be useless as an axe.

As we have seen, commodity money played a vital part in the history of the colonies in North America. Metal coins were very scarce. Most immigrants brought very little metallic coin with them, and the exporting of coin from Great Britain later became forbidden. A profitable business developed in smuggling Spanish coin but this was not sufficient to meet the demand. The use of commodities came about because the economy of the colonies was in many respects a "closed" one. Each community, and in fact almost each household, was "sufficient unto itself." Travel was limited and so there was little need for "money" to buy from others. It was easier to make use of items such as

Opposite: Picture reproduced from the book *The Story of America* (by permission of *Reader's Digest.*)

corn, hides, tobacco, ammunition and other common and useful items than to use a "money" that was often unavailable.

Metallic Money

Metallic money did not have to be coins. Some primitive tribes used various forms of metals, for example the drum money used by the people of Alor. Another form of metallic money was used by the people of Ethiopia. Warriors have been found armed only with spears but carrying quantities of rifle cartridges of various calibers, apparently a form of metallic money to them. In Borneo, bronze guns and cannons were used as a medium of exchange even in the early years of the twentieth century.

The time when metallic coins of a given weight were adopted as a means of completing transactions is lost in the uncertainty of ancient records. There is evidence that Egypt used copper, usually in the form of rings, to pay for goods. Historians speculate that during the third millennium the use of copper and some gold in various forms might have been used in addition to the more common measure of value, such as grain. It seems fairly clear from available records that true coins of silver, copper or gold did not come to Egypt until the invasion by Persia in 525 B.C. Still later, Alexander in 322 B.C., introduced coins but the Egyptians were reluctant to adopt them.

Babylonia and Assyria in the valley of the Tigris and Euphrates rivers were much more advanced than the Egyptians in the use of metallic money. Records indicate that at the time of the First Dynasty of Babel, 2225–1926 B.C., a monetary system using metallic money was well established. However, it fell to the people of Cappadocia, a part of the Assyrian empire, to produce the first official, state-stamped pieces of metal for monetary purposes. There is evidence that this was well established by 2250 B.C., 1500 years before the King of Lydia began stamping gold ingots with his seal.

It remained for the Greeks and the Romans to further refine the use of metallic coins. In Caesar's day, the Roman coin was well established throughout the known world. The Biblical account of Jesus' reply to the question of "should the Jews pay tribute to Caesar?" emphasizes the fact that the Roman coins bore the inscription of Caesar—a mark of authority and probably genuineness.

In our review of the use of metals for money we skip quickly over the next several hundred years to the time of the settling of the Americas. By that time metallic money was well established in most European countries. We will explore their use more in subsequent chapters.

Paper Money

The development of paper money is much less romantic and varied. Not only was paper very scarce and highly valued for other purposes, but the laborious task of printing probably delayed the use of paper money or currency as we call it today. Some students of paper money claim that the origin of paper money goes back to the clay tablets of Babylon, about 2500 B.C. On these tablets were written due bills and receipts. Others claim that since both paper and printing were invented in China, some documents resembling paper money were first produced in that country. Marco Polo, returning from his thirteenth-century voyage to China, reported that paper money was in use there. He also reported that Emperor Kubla Kahn, in A.D. 1273, issued notes in mulberry bark paper, bearing the red seal of Kubla and signatures of his treasurers. Very little counterfeiting occurred during Kubla Kahn's reign because when apprehended, the offenders were immediately executed. His paper currency also enjoyed full legal tender—it had to be accepted on any occasion—and those refusing to accept it were imprisoned or executed.

The earliest specimen of paper money known to exist today is the Kwan, a Chinese note issued during the Ming Dynasty (A.D. 1360–1399). It is about the size of a sheet of typewriter paper.

In the Middle Ages when travel became more common and trade began to develop extensively between nations, metal coins, particularly in large amounts, became burdensome and too heavy to carry from place to place. To overcome this obstacle, goldsmiths, merchants, and money lenders began to accept deposits of coins left for safekeeping and issue receipts. Later, such notes were issued in negotiable form and payable to the bearer. This custom grew in popularity and gradually the receipts were transferred from one person to another in payment of debts, instead of withdrawing the coin. This was the forerunner of paper money.

Another paper money as we know it today was issued in Sweden in about 1656 when the government authorized the establishment of a bank and it issued paper currency.

So much for the early history of money. In subsequent chapters we will look more closely at modern forms of money.

Chapter Two
Coins as Money

Early Coins

"I've got spurs that jingle jangle" go the words of a popular song in the 1940s. Alfred Lord Tennyson, hundreds of years earlier put it this way in his *Locksley Hall*, "But the jingling of the guinea helps the hurt that honor feels."

Little boys and men usually have coins in their pockets that jingle and give them a small sense of affluence and security.

Certain coins have been associated with the life of many men. George Washington was reported to have thrown a silver dollar across the Potomac River. This story seems to have developed because of activities during George's boyhood when he engaged in athletic contests with his friends, including throwing stones across the Rappahannock River, which bordered on the Washington estate. The large Spanish dollar was then in circulation and because of its weight, it is conceivable that he could have thrown it a long distance if so inclined. But George Washington was a conservative and thrifty person and it is questionable that he would have wasted a silver dollar.

John D. Rockefeller (1836–1937), the great business magnate and financier, frequently carried a pocket full of dimes in his later years which he delighted to give to people. This caused some uninformed persons to refer to him as "stingy" or "the old skin-flint." But this was grossly untrue as he was one of the world's greatest philanthropists. Out of his immense fortune he distributed about half a billion dollars in well-considered gifts for educational, scientific and other worthy endowments and foundations.

One of the most sought-after coins by coin collectors is the Indian head penny. This coin was redesigned in 1859 and a representation of an Indian girl was adopted on the obverse side of the coin. The picture is really that of a Caucasian head in Indian head dress. Records indicate that James B. Longacre, a famous designer at that time, used a young Caucasian girl as the model — some claim the model was his twelve-year-old daughter.

We noted in the previous chapter that metallic coins were well established in Europe by the time of the discovery of the Americas. Gold and silver had

A widely circulated coin in the world during the 17th and 18th centuries was the Spanish dollar. Many of these were minted in Mexico, and were sometimes called "columnarios," "dos mundos" or "mundos." Spanish dollars minted after 1771 carried a shield in place of the two worlds in the center. These coins were also called "pillar dollars" because of the two columns on the face of the coin. (Photo courtesy of *Coin World*.)

become the most cherished metals for coins. Much of the exploration of the New World was in search of these precious metals. One of the most sought-after and widely circulated coins was the Spanish gold dollar. These Spanish dollars were known as "pieces of eight" because each dollar was worth eight small Spanish coins known as "reales." One reale equaled twelve and one-half cents and was also known as a "bit." Some writers claim that because of the lack of reales to make change, the colonists sometimes cut these Spanish dollars into fractional parts: a quarter section of the dollar became "two bits," a half section "four bits," and three-fourths section "six bits," terms still used today.

We have looked at early uses of some coins. It is not our purpose now to delve into all of the incidents and reasons regarding the evolution of coins, but we will explore a few of the more interesting facts.

Following the development of coins by the Greeks, Romans and the Chinese from the third century B.C. to about 200 A.D., most nations or realms devised a coin for use in their transactions with other nations as well as to expedite trade within their own borders. It is interesting that monarchs frequently resorted to debasing the coin as resources, for their production became limited. Governments of every kind seemed to accept this as a means of maintaining their wealth. Evidence of such action in the United States is seen in the calling in of all gold coin in 1935 and fixing the price of gold at $35 per ounce. Then, in the 1960s and 1970s, we steadily reduced the amount of gold needed as collateral to our currency and finally eliminated it completely.

Early coins were often made of almost pure gold or silver. The ancient Greeks were probably the first to make coins of pure metal using gold or silver or "electrum"—a combination of gold and silver. However after the conquest of Greece by the Romans, the precious metal content of coins was steadily reduced. It is reported that as long as two centuries before the fall of Rome, coins were debased to the extent that they contained less than 2 percent gold.

Copper was usually the metal used to reduce the gold or silver content of coin; some lead and later zinc were also used. Nickel is used in some modern coins. The softness of gold and silver in their pure form causes rapid wear from abrasion, and copper has a tendency to oxidize and absorb acid from handling.

Subsidiary coins—those of lower values such as our nickels and pennies—generally consisted of copper. In France after the revolution of 1789 copper was so scarce that the church bells were melted down to provide copper for coins. It was in France that a mixture of metals was found that resisted the wear of circulation. This combination of metals was used later by most nations of the world. The secret: copper 95 percent, tin 4 percent and zinc 1 percent.

Coins in Colonial America

Leaving a more detailed discussion of coins to the numismatic specialists, we jump ahead to the time of the American colonies, particularly the thirteen colonies that later became the United States. Arriving from England or the European continent, immigrants usually had few coins, partly because most of the colonists were poor and also because the European countries and England took a dim view of coin leaving their shores. As a result, the colonists made use of coins from any source possible. As mentioned earlier, the Spanish dollar was eagerly sought and was held in high esteem. English coins also were circulated but used mostly for buying goods from the homeland.

Attempts by the colonists to set up their own mints ended when the British Crown ordered them closed. A few coins were struck and one that received considerable publicity was the "pine tree" coin struck by a mint in Boston. It bore the picture of a pine tree on one side and the number 1652 on the obverse side. Six-pence and three-pence pieces and willow tree and oak tree coins also were struck at this mint from 1653–1692. Counterfeiting of coins was rampant, not only in the colonies but in England and the Continent. In fact, one of the punishments for counterfeiting in England was to send the guilty parties to the colonies. Most of the colonists handled very few coins, so they were not familiar with the genuine and easily accepted counterfeits. In England during the 1700s counterfeiting was punishable by death, but the practice was so widespread that one justice of the peace wrote to the Governor and complained, "What can a justice do when the whole country combines against him.... My property is destroyed day and night and durst not say ill done."

In his book *Counterfeiting in Colonial America,* Kenneth Scott tells of the arrival of a ship in Maryland with a number of coiners aboard. A few days after they landed the *Maryland Gazette* warned its readers that already counterfeit dollars and shillings were in circulation.

During the time following the Declaration of Independence and up to the adoption of the Constitution, a number of state legislatures authorized the issuance of coins. The struggle by the infant nation to establish a sound, acceptable coin is a fascinating story.

United States Coinage

Every new nation wants to establish its own coins for prestige and also to facilitate financing of governmental operations and private trade. The thirteen colonies, later to become the United States, had an even more urgent need. They were desperate to finance the revolt against England. The continental currency that was issued had no backing and despite urging by officials, coins were hoarded and the currency fell in disrepute, sending prices higher and higher. The critical need for fighting the war is illustrated by the following communication from General Schuyler to General Washington:

> I have this moment received a letter from General Wooster, of the 1st instant. He says not a word relative to Quebec; complains of a want of specie, and indeed, nor without reason as he is greatly distressed, the Canadians absolutely refusing to take our paper moeny.... The difficulty of procuring specie is such, that I fear the most fatal consequences from the want of it in Canada.

After the war was won and the fledgling government of the United States struggled to organize, the question of a mint to strike coins was raised. Don Taxay in his *The U.S. Mint and Coinage* (pp. 4–5) points out that there is no reference to a mint in the year 1776. The 1776 "Continental currency" coin probably was a private issue. This coin, known as the "Fugio" coin had on its obverse side the words "Continental Currency 1776" and "Fugio MIND YOUR BUSINESS." At the upper left, the sun's rays strike a sundial. The reverse side showed a perpetual chain with each link inscribed with the name of a colony. In the center was the legend: "AMERICAN CONGRESS: WE ARE ONE." Whether or not this was an official coin is not certain. There is considerable evidence that it was, but little in the official records to support it.

As the government attempted to bring about order to the medium of exchange in the young Republic there was much discussion and difference of opinion as to the best coin, the metal to be used, the engraving and wording on the coins, and whether or not the striking of the coins should be contracted, or a mint established. One of the most significant decisions revolved around the choice of a decimal system or a system of value patterned after the English pound, shilling, etc. The use of the term "dollar" had been well established; it was in common use not only in the colonies but much of western Europe. The word comes from the Joachimsthaler, a coin first minted in 1519 in the Valley of St. Joachim, Bohemia. These Joachimsthalers were later called "thalers," a name given by the Germans to a large-sized silver coin. The English named them "dollars." Since the Spanish "dollar" was well known to the colonists, this name was adopted for the principal unit of money of the new Republic.

There are many versions of the story concerning the origin of the $ (dollar) sign. The most widely accepted explanation is that it developed as a result of evolution, independently in different places, of the Spanish or Mexican "P's" for pesos or plastres, or the Spanish dollars. Some claim that the "S" gradually came to be written over the "P," developing a close resemblance to the $ mark, which eventually evolved. It was widely used before the adoption of the United States dollar in 1785.

Many nations had their coins struck by others on a contract basis. Lacking capital, this seemed like a logical choice for the United States. However, there was much sentiment for authorizing a mint. Thomas Jefferson, Benjamin Franklin, Alexander Hamilton and Robert Morris, an able merchant from Philadelphia and the first superintendent of finance, were among those who took active parts in developing the new coins. It was Jefferson who finally won the argument for a decimal system as opposed to one patterned after the English system.

An interesting sidelight to the evolution of U.S. coins is seen in a communication to Congress in 1781 by William Barton, an attorney from Philadelphia. He suggested that the melting down of coins be prohibited by law and that Congress should have the right to coin money (this later became part of the Constitution).

The struggle to find a suitable and acceptable system of coins persisted for several years. Morris in 1782 proposed a system that included the following units: mark, 250 grains fine silver; quint, 125 grains fine silver; cent, 25 grains fine silver; eight and five, the last two not given weights. This complicated arrangement of units was an attempt to adjust to the various values then in use in the colonies. Each had its own value for the Spanish dollar and for English coins. This was not an easy environment in which to encourage trade.

The Morris plan was sent to Congress and on February 21, 1782. Congress approved the establishment of a mint and directed the superintendent (Morris) to prepare and report "a plan for the establishing of and conducting of same."

Morris's enthusiasm and that of his coworker, Benjamin Dudley, an expert assayist, apparently caused him to misread the directive of Congress to "prepare and report," and they proceeded to begin construction of a mint in Philadelphia in an unoccupied building on Fourth Street near Vine. This building had previously served as the Dutch Reformed Church. Morris continued with the construction and the striking of specimen coins during the next year and a half. Congress, however, was in no mood to place its approval of the project, and in January 1784 the Morris plan was referred to a new committee which included Thomas Jefferson.

At this point, Jefferson assumed leadership and pointed out the difficulty of using the units suggested by Morris. He stated in his own colorful language that it was "defective" in two of the three requisites of a money unit. One, it was inconvenient to ordinary money transactions. Second, it was neither equal to nor near any of the known coins of value. Here is part of his statement:

> I know of no unit which can be proposed in competition with the dollar, but the pound; but what is the pound? 1547 grains of fine silver in Georgia; 1289 grains in Virginia, Connecticut, Rhode Island, Massachusetts and New Hampshire; 1031¼ grains in Maryland, Delaware, Pennsylvania and New Jersey; 99¾ grains in North Carolina and New York. Which of these shall we adopt? To which state give that preeminence of which all are so jealous? And upon which impose the difficulties of a new estimate for their coin, their cattle and other commodities? Or shall we hang the pound sterling as a common badge about all their necks? This contains 1718¾ grains of pure silver.

The First Mint Established

This appeared to settle the question of the unit but still no action was taken to establish a mint. On May 10, 1785, John Jay submitted a proposal to Congress and while his proposal was not used, it did stimulate some action, and a "Grand Committee" was appointed with thirteen members. On July 6, 1785, Congress unanimously approved the recommendations of the Grand Committee including that the unit be the dollar, the smallest coin be of copper of which 200 should pass for one dollar, and that several pieces increase in decimal ratio.

But the game wasn't over yet. Several reports were made to Congress but by 1788 there was still no mint. Passage of the Constitution in June 1788 called for action as it stated among other things that "No State shall coin money, omit bills of credit, make anything but gold and silver coin a tender in payment of debts." However, there was still no legislation to establish a mint, and many continued to believe it would be cheaper to contract the striking of the coins.

In late 1791, specimen half-dollars and some cents were struck and distributed to members of Congress. About this time it became known to Jefferson and Thomas Paine that the business of coinage was a very lucrative business and hence the competition by those capable of producing coin to gain a contract. This stimulated much support in the Congress for the establishment of a mint under government ownership and supervision. Debate in the Senate in early 1792 proposed such action and also described the inscription to be used on the coins. One of the descriptions of the coins is of particular interest: One side was to show the head of the president of the United States, with this to change with the succession of presidents. The reverse side was to have the eagle and the words "UNITED STATES OF AMERICA."

When the sample coins were shown to Congress and to President Washington, he took strong exception to the use of the head of the president. Republican John Paige's statement reflects what probably was the feeling of Washington and many other leaders. He pointed out that monarchies for centuries had used coins to show their power and time of their reign and mentioned the fact that the Jews paid tribute to Caesar with coins bearing his likeness. He added,

> . . . [We] have no occasion for this aid to history nor any pretense to call the money of the United States the money of our President. . . . I am certain it will be more agreeable to the citizens of the United States to see the head of Liberty on their coin, than the heads of Presidents. However well pleased they might be with the head of the great man now their President . . . they may have no great reason to be pleased with some of his successors; as to him, they have his busts, his pictures everywhere, historians are daily celebrating his fame and Congress has voted him a monument. A further compliment they need not pay him, especially when it may be said, that no Republic has paid such a compliment to their Chief Magistrate and wound the feelings of many friends and gratify our enemies.

After much debate, especially in the Conference Committee, on March 2, 1792, the long-awaited act establishing a mint and regulating the coins of the United States was enacted. The Philadelphia Mint was established on April 2, 1792, under the bill passed by Congress and signed by President Washington. Among other things the act authorized the following denominations:

Metal	Denomination	Value
Gold	Eagle	$10.00
	Half Eagle	$ 5.00
	Quarter Eagle	$ 2.50
Silver	Dollar	$ 1.00
	Half-Dollar	$ .50
	Quarter Dollar	$ .25
	Dime	$ .10
	Half Dime	$ .05
Copper	Cent	$ .01
	Half Cent	$ .005

The copper coins were not legal tender, which led to their being ignored by the public and other coins were substituted, such as the English halfpence, foreign and domestic counterfeits and miscellaneous tokens, all of which circulated freely. The act also fixed the death penalty for any mint employee who debased the coinage for profit or other fraudulent purpose.

Leaving the intriguing and sometimes humorous debate over the establishment of a mint, let us move on to the sequence of coinage since that time. It is good to remember that some very basic principles were set in place as the fragile government of the new Republic struggled to set its course in history. The strong abhorrence of any kind of monarchy is one; establishment of our own mint which today provides coinage for many nations is another. Perhaps of equal importance was the selection of the dollar and the decimal system of coins that we find so easy and useful today.

The first coins minted at the Philadelphia Mint were silver "half dismes," which was how "dime" was then spelled. Silver for making the first batch of these coins is said to have been furnished by George and Martha Washington from their own household silver service, to the value of about one hundred dollars. According to an old story, the portrait on these coins represents Martha Washington, copied in profile from John Trumbull's painting. George Washington is also said to have donated a copper tea kettle in 1793 for making the first cent pieces. The nation's first cents and half cents were struck in 1793; they were copper and about the size of present-day quarters and nickels. A silver half dime, half-dollar, and dollar were added in 1794, and the next year the eagle $10 gold coin and half eagle appeared. At that time, the eagle was the gold and the dollar the silver monetary unit. The motto *E. Pluribus Unum* was first used on the half eagle of 1795. The next year our first quarters and dimes were issued.

Gold Coinage

Gold coins were minted in the United States from 1792 to 1933; during this period the mint coined gold totaling $4,526 million. As provided by the act of 1792, eagles became the standard denomination of gold coin and with half eagles and double eagles, were the first gold coins struck. The act of March 3, 1849, authorized coinage of double eagles and $1 gold pieces, and the act of February 21, 1853, provided for the mintage of a $3 gold piece. However, only about 20 million $1 gold coins and less than 1 million $3 coins were minted before authorization for these denominations ended in 1890. Approximately 20 million quarter eagles were minted before the authorization was withdrawn in 1930. Coinage of gold was prohibited by the Gold Reserve Act of 1934. Existing stocks of gold coin were returned to the Treasury and formed into gold bars; thus ended 142 years of gold coinage in the United States.

During the early 1980s investment in gold coins became popular partly as a means of offsetting possible losses in other investments and also to satisfy the desire of many individuals to hold this intrinsically valuable coin. Demand for the South African Krugerrand and the Canadian Maple Leaf coins (both gold coins) raised their market price well above the value of the gold content. Moreover, this price fluctuated considerably as market conditions changed. They were often promoted as a hedge against inflation. Sentiment in favor of placing an embargo on South African goods because of that government's policy of apartheid caused President Reagan to issue a presidential order on October 11, 1985, forbidding the importation of the Krugerrand.

As Americans continued to demand gold coin, in December 1985, Congress passed Public Law 99–185 entitled The Gold Bullion Act of 1985. This bill authorized the minting of legal tender gold bullion coins. These were not intended as a medium of circulation but as an investment.

The coins became available through coin dealers and financial institutions in early November 1986. They were priced at the then-market value of their gold content plus a small premium. This price fluctuates with changes in the market price of gold.

There are four denominations of the coin. The one-ounce coin has a face value of $50, the half-ounce $25, the quarter-ounce $10 and the tenth-ounce $5. All of the coins are .9167 fine gold. Congress specified that the coins have on the obverse side a design symbolic of liberty and on the reverse side, a design representing a family of eagles, with the male carrying an olive branch and flying above a nest containing a female eagle and hatchlings. This design symbolizes the unity and family tradition of America. There are minor refinements to the Saint-Gaudens double eagle Liberty on the gold coins. The most noticeable is the increase in the number of stars around the border to fifty. Roman numerals will be used to designate the year of issue. Augustus Saint-Gaudens' initials appear on the design. More detailed information on these coins is shown in the Appendix.

Silver Coinage

Silver had been coined, in some form, since the act of 1792. Silver dollars were coined until 1873, although their weight was reduced slightly in 1837. Coinage of silver dollars was prohibited by the act of 1873, but authorization was restored by the act of 1878 and production continued until 1935.

The Coinage acts of 1965 and 1970 authorized discontinuance of the use of silver in our coins. All dimes, quarters, half-dollars and dollars now produced for regular circulation are cupro-nickel-clad metal.

What the people want in coins they eventually get. In 1985 Congress passed the Liberty Coin Act of July 9, 1985. This act provided for the striking and issuing of silver-dollar coins to meet the demand of the public. The new coins were to have a symbol of liberty on the obverse side and an eagle on the reverse side. To comply with the act, the obverse side of the new silver coin bears the Walking Liberty design by Adolph A. Weinman, which was formerly used on the half-dollar from 1916 to 1947. The reverse side bears a heraldic eagle designed by mint sculptor-engraver John Mercanti. In this design the eagle is shown with a shield holding arrows in one talon and an olive branch in the other. Unlike earlier U.S. silver dollars that are 1½ inches in diameter and contain a little over three quarters of an ounce of fine silver, the new coins are slightly larger in diameter and contain one ounce of fine silver. The minting date is shown in Arabic numbers. Additional details are shown in the Appendix.

Present Coinage

Disregarding bullion coins, all but one currently minted coins honor past presidents; the one exception is the Susan B. Anthony dollar. Authorized United States coins presently issued and the likeness of our presidents appearing on the obverse (face) are: cent (Lincoln); nickel (Jefferson); dime (Roosevelt); quarter (Washington); half-dollar (Kennedy) and dollar (Eisenhower). All coins issued in the United States are token coins in that their value as money exceeds the value of their metallic content.

The world-wide interest in President Kennedy and his tragic death warrant more detail about the coin struck in his honor. The following quote from the Treasury Department's press release gives details of the coin design and interesting information regarding the use of the Presidential Seal on coins.

John Fitzgerald Kennedy was inaugurated President of the United States January 20, 1961, and served not quite three full years of his term of office. His untimely death on November 22, 1963 resulted in such outpouring of public sentiment that President Johnson, on December 10, 1963, sent to the Congress legislation authorizing the Treasury Department to mint new 50-cent pieces bearing the likeness of his predecessor.

Legislative authority is necessary in order to change a coin design which has not been in effect for the 25-year period required by law. Congress gave its overwhelming approval to the President's recommendation and on December 30, 1963, the bill was signed into law directing the Mint to proceed with the production of the new design. The half dollar was selected because this would add another Presidential portrait to a coin of regular issue.

In the center of the obverse, or face of the coin, is a strong but simple bust of the late President, facing left. Above, and around the border is the word LIBERTY. Just below the bust is the motto IN GOD WE TRUST, which appears on all United States coins of current issue. The date appears around the border at the bottom of the coin.

The Presidential Coat of Arms forms the motif for the reverse, or back of the coin. It is the central part of the Presidential Seal, the only difference being that the words SEAL OF THE PRESIDENT OF THE UNITED STATES have been removed and in their place are inscriptions required by law to appear on all United States coins: the words UNITED STATES OF AMERICA, above, around the border, and the denomination, HALF DOLLAR, around the bottom of the border. Other requirements already incorporated in the Coat of Arms are the eagle, and E PLURIBUS UNUM, which appears on the ribbon above the eagle's head.

The Kennedy coin had its beginnings when official sculptors were engaged in preparing a new medal for the historic series of Presidential pieces manufactured in bronze for sale to the public. Gilroy Roberts, nationally known Chief Sculptor of the United States Mint, and a member of the Philadelphia staff for many years, worked on the likeness of the President, studying first many photographs to capture the character and personality of his subject. He then selected a single portrait and commenced placing his concept in a preliminary model. During the final stages, Mr. Roberts called at the White House and studied the President at work, at which time he completed his model.

After the President's death, when the decision was reached to honor him on a United States coin, the Roberts portrait was adapted from the medal, lowered in relief and simplified for use on the smaller scale necessary for a coin.

Frank Gasparro, also a veteran member of the Philadelphia staff, executed the reverse of the Presidential medal. The Coat of Arms of the President of the United States, an integral part of this design, was chosen as the companion side for the half dollar. Gasparro also designed the Lincoln Memorial side of the current cent.

The Coat of Arms depicts the American Eagle holding in its right talon an olive branch of peace, and in the left talon, arrows for defense. Symbolism derived from the Thirteen Original States governs the number of olive leaves, berries, arrows, stars and cloud puffs. The upper part of the flag or shield upon the breast of the eagle represents the Congress binding the Colonies into an entity. The vertical stripes complete the motif of the Flag of the United States. Each State of the Nation is represented in the 50-star amulet which rings the whole. The theme of the device is punctuated by the motto E PLURIBUS UNUM, which appears on the ribbon above the eagle's head. Translated "One out of Many," it refers to the unity of the States and the strength of our Nation.

The Presidential Seal originated during the Administration of President Rutherford B. Hayes, apparently as a rendering of the Great Seal of the United States. There was no known basis in law for the Coat of Arms and the Seal which had been used by Presidents since 1880 and which was reproduced on the Presidential Flag. President Harry S. Truman, when he signed the Executive order of October 25, 1945, containing the official description, established for the first time a legal definition of the President's Coat of Arms and his Seal. According to heraldic custom, the eagle on a Coat of Arms, unless otherwise specified in the heraldic description, is always made to face to its own right. There is no explanation for the eagle facing to its own left in the case of the President's Coat of Arms. To conform to heraldic custom, and since there was no authority other than usage for the former

Presidential Coat of Arms, President Franklin D. Roosevelt had asked that it be redesigned. The designs reached Washington after the President's death.

In the new Coat of Arms, Seal and Flag, the eagle not only faces to its right — the direction of honor — but also toward the olive branches of peace which it holds in its right talon. Formerly, the eagle faced toward the arrows in its left talon — arrows, symbolic of war.

The Kennedy half dollar is not a commemorative coin. Such Commemorative coins are authorized by special acts of Congress, manufactured in limited quantities and sold at a profit by the private organizations sponsoring the issues. The Kennedy coin was being made for regular distribution and the design will remain in effect for 25 years, as prescribed by law, unless the Congress authorizes a change in the interim. It takes the place of the Franklin design, which first appeared in 1948.

Despite the Treasury's announcement that the coin would be a part of the regular coin supply for fifteen years, it quickly became a collector's item and was eagerly sought world-wide. Also, the public, long without a half-dollar coin, declined to resume their habit of carrying the larger coin. The demand for the coin as collector's item virtually prevented it from circulating freely. By 1970, the mint had issued 1.2 billion Kennedy half-dollars but they still did not become a part of general circulation. As with other coins, the silver content was such that with the rising price of silver it became necessary to shift to the cupro-nickel-clad design for the Kennedy half. The coin still was not accepted by the public.

For many years after the disappearance of the silver dollar from the coin scene — they were kept as collector's items or held for the value of the silver in them — there was a demand for a dollar coin. Most people thought of a silver dollar but the price of silver made that out of the question. In addition to the sentimental wish for a silver dollar, the economics of the situation brought additional pressure for a dollar coin. After all, a coin would last for years while a dollar bill in currency had a life of not more than a year. The cost of printing millions of bills annually was a major item in the cost of providing coins and currency. If a dollar coin could be substituted for the paper dollar, the savings would be substantial.

The 1970 coinage legislation provided for the minting of a dollar coin bearing the likeness of former president Dwight D. Eisenhower. This was the first dollar coin minted since 1935, and it was the first time a president's image had been used on a dollar coin. About 150 million of the coins were minted with 40 percent silver for a sale at premium prices. The balance was cupro-nickel-clad dollar coins. General circulation was started in 1971. The following quote from the Treasury's press release provides additional information about the Eisenhower dollar:

> Frank Gasparro, the U.S. Mint's chief sculptor and engraver, designed the front and back of the Eisenhower dollar coin.

He began working on the obverse drawing for the coin in the spring of 1969 and settled on using a profile of the former President and General of the Army because of a fond and lasting recollection of strength and character he perceived when first he saw Eisenhower.

Mr. Gasparro was standing curbside on Fifth Avenue in New York City on June 20, 1945, one of the estimated 4,000,000 citizens who joined in a tumultuous welcome home and victory parade for the famous Five Star General after the close of World War II.

Mr. Gasparro got only a fleeting glimpse of the Supreme Commander of the Allied Armies in Europe as he rode by. He carried his image of Eisenhower's courage and character back to work with him at the Philadelphia Mint and immediately made a profile drawing suitable to cut directly in steel and capture the strong facial features that so deeply impressed him.

When Mr. Gasparro was asked to design the Eisenhower dollar coin, he studied his first drawing of Eisenhower and some 30 other pictures before sketching his design for the obverse of the coin. He engraved his initials, F.G., in the base of the bust.

Also appearing on the obverse are the word, "Liberty" and the national motto "In God We Trust" as required by Public Law, as well as the year of coinage.

Mr. Gasparro began work on the reverse of the Eisenhower coin in October of 1969.

An amendment to the coinage bill, first introduced by Representative Bob Casey (D. Tex.) provided that the reverse design be symbolic of the Apollo 11 flight honoring the exploits of our country's astronauts and the first landing on the moon.

The Congress deemed the Apollo 11 insignia particularly appropriate for the Eisenhower coin because of space programs begun under the administration of President Eisenhower.

Title 31 U.S. Code, Section 324, requires that an eagle appear on the design of coins in denominations of a quarter and above. The Apollo 11 spaceship christened "The Eagle," landed on Tranquility Base on July 21, 1969. The majestic bird swooping in for a landing was adopted to represent the Apollo 11 mission.

Mr. Gasparro's rendition of the Apollo 11 insignia shows the bald eagle landing on the crater-pocked surface of the moon, an olive branch clutched in both claws.

The receding earth appears above the eagle's head and below the motto "E Pluribus Unum," required by statute on all U.S. coins. The 13 stars represent the first states of the Union. Circling the coin are the words "United States of America" and "one dollar." The designer's initials, F.G., appear at the right below the eagle's tail feathers.

Much attention was given to the "character" of the emblematic drawing of the symbolic eagle of Apollo 11 landing on the moon. Mint Director Mary T. Brooks requested the artist to draw "a peaceful eagle." Mr. Gasparro describes his rendition as "a pleasant-looking eagle."

President Nixon, Treasury Department and Mint Officials, and the Fine Arts Commission approved the sketches Mr. Gasparro submitted for the obverse and reverse designs of the Eisenhower coin.

Subsequently the plastilene models (modeling wax) were approved. Eugene Rossides, the Treasury's Assistant Secretary for Enforcement and Operations, and Mint Director Mary T. Brooks then met with Mrs. Dwight D. Eisenhower and secured her approval of the design of the coin. Mrs. Eisenhower was especially pleased with the portrait of her late husband.

Again, the whims and habits of the general public failed to measure up to the Treasury's expectations. The Eisenhower dollars were quickly stashed away as collector's items and they soon virtually disappeared from circulation. They were too large for convenience in men's pockets and the cupro-nickel coin was not attractive. The public was accustomed to a "real" silver dollar to give at Christmas time and as keepsakes. The "cheap" clad dollar was a far cry from the "cartwheels" of earlier years and was not accepted.

But the clamor for a dollar coin persisted, fueled by sentiment as well as the economics of trying to substitute a coin for dollar bills.

In October 1978 Congress authorized discontinuing the issuing of the Eisenhower dollar and directed that a new dollar coin bearing the image of Susan B. Anthony be minted. This was the first time that the portrait of a woman other than a symbolic one appeared on a circulating coin. The selection of Susan B. Anthony coincided with a strong movement at the time for greater recognition of women's rights. This action acknowledged the contribution of Miss Anthony to the women's rights movement. Miss Anthony was an early crusader for equal rights for women and a pioneer in the drive to win for women the right to vote. In 1920 her life-long work culminated in the ratification of the Nineteenth Amendment to the Constitution giving nationwide suffrage to women.

The reverse side of the new coin carried the Apollo 11 spacecraft — the same design that had been on the Eisenhower dollar. It was anticipated that the new coin would last at least fifteen years and be a welcome addition to the coins available to the public. The new coin was smaller than a half-dollar coin but slightly larger than the quarter. To help blind persons "feel" the difference between these three coins, an irregular ridge was forged just inside the edge. The coin was launched with great fanfare and publicity. Millions were purchased by Federal Reserve banks and sold to commercial banks. The public's reaction was favorable at first but it soon became evident that the difference in size between the quarter, half-dollar and the dollar was not adequate for ready identification. Soon the public said, "It's just like a quarter." Clerks refused to accept them or if they did they put them in a special place in the cash register and took them out of circulation. Within a few years they had virtually disappeared from circulation.

Since the establishment of the first United States Mint in 1792, United States coins of various kinds, denominations, and sizes have been authorized, issued, and discontinued, such as the half cent, large cent, two-cent piece, three-cent piece, twenty-cent piece, and half dime. Also discontinued are gold coins in denominations of $1, $2.50 ("Quarter Eagle"); $3, $4 (known as

"Stella" and issued only in 1879 and 1880); $5 ("Half Eagle"); $10 ("Eagle"); $20 ("Double Eagle") issued at various times and used from 1795 to 1933.

Commemorative Coins

These are coins that commemorate a historical event, an anniversary, or a person. They are authorized for worthy causes by special acts of Congress, produced in limited quantities, and sold at a premium by private organizations sponsoring the issues. They have been struck in silver and gold (mostly in half-dollars) from 1892–1954. The first commemorative coin was minted in 1892 to help finance the World's Columbian Exposition in Chicago. Since that time, fifty different types of such coins have been issued including forty-eight half-dollars, a quarter-dollar and a one-dollar denomination. Because they sell at a premium, few have circulated as regular coin. Some issues, picked at random as illustrations, are: a half-dollar issued in 1921 to commemorate the 100th anniversary of the admission of Missouri into the Union; a half-dollar issued 1934–1938 to commemorate the 100th anniversary of Texas's independence from Mexico in 1834; a half-dollar issued in 1936 to commemorate the Battle of Gettysburg; and the Washington-Carver half-dollar issued 1951–1954 in honor of Booker T. Washington and George Washington Carver. This coin was the first ever to honor any black Americans; the purpose of the issue was to help raise funds for the building of a memorial.

More recently, the mint struck coins to celebrate the 200th anniversary of the Declaration of Independence. While these were placed in circulation they were essentially a commemorative coin. In 1976 a dollar, a half-dollar and a quarter were minted and offered to the public. They were 40 percent silver and virtually flawless in design and production. The reverse side of each coin carried a symbol of independence and liberty. The dollar coin depicts Independence Hall, the half-dollar a drummer and the quarter the Liberty Bell. These commemorative coins were made from special coin blanks and struck twice by highly polished dies to give a mirror-like surface. Coins with the same design but in cupro–nickel-clad material were circulated for some time but most were hoarded as collector's items because of the special date—1776–1976—stamped below the portrait.

"In God We Trust"

"In God We Trust" first appeared on a coin of the United States in 1864, and owes its presence largely to the increased religious sentiment existing during the Civil War. Salmon P. Chase, then secretary of the treasury, received a number of appeals from devout persons throughout the country urging that the Deity be recognized suitably on our coins similar to that commonly found on the coins of other nations. Accordingly, on November 20, 1861, Secretary Chase in a letter to the director of the mint at Philadelphia directing such a device, stated that "No nation can be strong except in the strength of God, or safe except in His defense."

The familiar form of the motto finally was decided upon, but its use has been interrupted and it has not appeared on all coins of all series. It first appeared on a new 2-cent piece in 1864. In 1866, double-eagle, eagle, and half-eagle gold coins and silver dollar, half-dollar and quarter-dollar pieces bearing the motto were introduced. The nickel five-cent piece bore the motto from 1866 to 1883, when it was dropped, and not restored until the introduction of the Jefferson nickel in 1938. It first appeared on the cent in 1909, and on the dime in 1916, and has continued in use on those coins since.

A law passed by the Eighty-fourth Congress and approved by the president on July 11, 1955, provides that "In God We Trust" shall appear on all United States paper currency and coins. One-dollar silver certificates bearing the inscription were made available to the public on October 1, 1957. This law applied to all currency issued by the United States government and by the twelve Federal Reserve banks. Any new series of currency issued since the passing of the law bears the legend "In God We Trust."

By joint resolution of the Eighty-fourth Congress and approved by the president on July 30, 1956, "In God We Trust" was declared to be the national motto of the United States.

How Coins Are Made and Stored

Any significant change in our currency and coin such as type, denomination, measurements, metallic content, weight, monetary standard, legal tender, and convertibility must be authorized by the Congress of the United States. Instructions from Congress are carried out by the Bureau of the Mint. The Bureau is a division of the United States Treasury Department and is headed by the director of the mint, whose offices are in Washington, D.C. The Bureau of the Mint has supervision over the following branch mints:

Philadelphia Mint. Has been in continuous operation since it first began striking coins in 1792.
Denver Mint. Authorized in 1862 but did not begin coinage operations until 1906.
San Francisco Mint. Established in 1854 and discontinued its coinage operations in 1955.

In the past, branch mints have also operated at Carson City, Nevada; Charlotte, North Carolina; Dahlonega, Georgia; and New Orleans, Louisiana. The Carson City Mint was in use from 1870 through 1893. The Charlotte and

Dahlonega mints produced only gold coins, and their operations were suspended in 1861 because of the Civil War; neither reopened. The New Orleans Mint was seized in 1861 by the Confederate government and operated for a time as a confederate mint. It was reopened in 1879 by the federal government and coinage operations were carried on until 1909, when they were finally discontinued.

Usually, the selection of coin designs is made by the director of the mint, with the approval of the Secretary of the Treasury. However, Congress sometimes prescribes or sets up guidelines for coin designs.

Portraits of United States presidents are on coins now being manufactured as follows:

> *Cent.* The Lincoln cent was the first portrait coin of a regular series minted by the United States. The occasion of the 100th anniversary of Lincoln's birth aroused sentiment sufficiently strong to overcome a long prevailing, popular prejudice against the use of portraits on coins. A new reverse design was adopted in 1959 in connection with the observance of the sesquicentennial of Lincoln's birth. The familiar likeness of Lincoln on the obverse remains unchanged.
>
> *Nickel.* Thomas Jefferson is honored on the 5-cent piece, using the design adopted in 1938.
>
> *Dime.* The likeness of Franklin D. Roosevelt appears on the dime design adopted in 1946.
>
> *Quarter.* As part of the bicentennial celebration of Washington's birth, held in 1932, Congress declared that the likeness of our first president should appear on the quarter dollar.
>
> *Half.* The John F. Kennedy likeness was placed on the half-dollar by an act of Congress approved December 30, 1963, and the first coins were released March 24, 1964.
>
> *Dollar.* On December 31, 1970, legislation approved by the Congress directed placement of the likeness of Dwight D. Eisenhower upon the obverse of the dollar coin, with a representation of the Apollo 11 insignia upon the reverse. On July 2, 1970, Congress approved a dollar coin with the likeness of Susan B. Anthony on the obverse side.

No change in the design of a coin may be made for twenty-five years after its adoption. An act of Congress would be necessary before the expiration of this period. There are no restrictions upon the length of time a design may remain in use upon expiration of the limitation set by law.

A world shortage of silver and the necessity of conserving this metal for industrial uses were the major factors behind the passage of the Coinage Act of 1965 which authorized the discontinuance of the use of silver in our coins. A bill signed by President Lyndon B. Johnson on July 23, 1954, provided for

Opposite: Rows of coining metal in coils are readied for processes which will convert them into millions of United States coins at the United States Mint, Philadelphia, PA. (Courtesy United States Treasury Department.)

the first major change in the United States coinage in more than a century. Silver was eliminated from the dime and the quarter and substantially reduced in the half-dollar. The 1970 coinage law provided for the removal of all silver from the half-dollar. The legislation passed in 1970 also provided for the removal of all silver from the dollar denomination and cupro-nickel-clad composition. All dimes, quarters, half-dollars and dollars now produced for regular circulation are cupro-nickel-clad metal.

The first step in coin manufacture is to prepare the alloy. By mixing certain metals, coins are made hard, strong and durable. For example, pure copper is a soft, weak metal; tin is even weaker and softer. If you mix nine parts of copper with one part of tin, the result is an alloy called bronze, which is hard and strong.

Our penny is an alloy of 95 percent copper and 5 percent zinc. Our five-cent piece is an alloy of 25 percent nickel and 75 percent copper, called cupronickel.

Alloys used in one-cent and five-cent pieces are made from accurately weighted and combined pure metals, melted in electric furnaces and poured into molds to form ingots. The ingots are then passed several times through rolling mills to reduce them to strips of the exact thickness needed. To keep the cupro-nickel pliable enough for rolling, it is run through an annealing furnace, washed and dried. The strips are then fed into high-speed punch presses which cut circular planchets or blanks of the proper size.

Planchets for the one-cent and five-cent coins are run through an edge-rolling machine which produces a raised rim on them. This helps to prevent the surface features of the coins from wearing away in normal use. With a single stroke, the coining press stamps the designs of both the obverse and reverse dies on the planchet.

Dimes, quarters, half-dollars, and dollars are made from strips composed of three layers of metal bonded together and rolled to the required thickness. The bonding process is called "cladding." The face is 75 percent copper and 25 percent nickel and the core is pure copper, which is visible on the edges of the coin. The three strips to be bonded are softened in large coil annealing furnaces, carefully cleaned, wire brushed, and rolled together under high pressure. The clad strip is then rolled to final blank thickness. From this point forward the manufacturing processes are almost the same as for the one-cent and five-cent coins. Edges of dimes, quarters, half-dollars and dollars are "reeded" as a part of the stamping operation. Reeding involves forcing the metal into grooves of the collar holding the coin, thus producing the milling on the rim. Milling prevents coins from being shaved without detection.

Opposite: A small portion of the coining presses at the United States Mint, Philadelphia, Pennsylvania is shown here, as an electric cart moves between rows carrying huge metal bins filled with struck coins, ready for bagging and shipment to the Federal Reserve Bank system. (Courtesy United States Treasury Department.)

After a final inspection, counting and weighing, the coins are put in canvas bags and stored pending shipment to the Federal Reserve banks and branches. Dimes, quarters, half-dollars and dollars are sacked $1,000 per bag for each denomination; nickels are sacked $200 per bag; and cents, $50 per bag. Dimes, quarters, half-dollars and dollars weigh approximately 50 pounds per bag; nickels approximately 44 pounds; and cents, approximately 34½ pounds.

The quantity of coins produced by the mints depends upon demand, which is especially great at certain times such as just before Christmas. The Federal Reserve offices ask the Bureau of the Mint to furnish coins they need to meet the demands of the commercial banks in their respective areas. The banks provide the Bureau with estimations of their requirements for the months ahead. These, and other factors, help the Bureau to determine the quantity of the various coin denominations to produce.

The volume of United States and foreign coins produced at the United States mints during the calendar year 1986 is shown in the Appendix.

The Bureau of the Mint is constantly making studies and evaluating the possibility of discontinuing a present coin or issuing new coins with a view toward effecting economies in production and better serving the nation's economy.

Chapter Three
Currency

Its Origins

The story is told of the preacher who, when the time came for the Sunday morning offering, admonished his congregation as follows: "I don't want to hear any of that jingling money, just the quiet sound of folding money."

Whether the story is true or not dollar amounts do grow faster when we use currency instead of coin. Today in the United States we accept currency (paper money) readily in payment for goods and services. In fact, if we are offered our change in coin in amounts over one dollar, the clerk usually apologizes for not having the correct paper money. Currency has the same respect in most modern countries.

It has not always been so. Only in recent history has currency enjoyed the confidence that we have in it today. There is no intrinsic value to the piece of paper we use for money. The value of the paper and ink in a twenty-dollar bill is less than three cents, and the cost of printing and distributing is measured in cents. There is no silver or gold behind our currency—you cannot take it to a bank or to the Federal Reserve Bank or the United States Treasury and get silver or gold in exchange. In a very real sense it is "token" money.

In an earlier chapter we commented on the early use of paper money. The Babylonians are reported to have used clay tablets on which to write due bills and receipts as early as 2500 B.C. This could be the earliest use of a form of "currency." Marco Polo found the Chinese Emperor Kubla Kahn using mulberry bark paper notes bearing his seal and signature in A.D. 1273. The oldest surviving specimen of paper money is the Kwan, a Chinese note issued between 1368 and 1399, during the Ming dynasty; this currency was about the size of typewriter paper.

As we mentioned earlier, substituting receipts for coin became quite common during the Middle Ages. Its use discouraged robbers and the receipts were more convenient to carry. People deposited their gold and silver and other coins with someone with a safe place to keep them and were issued receipts in return. As long as the person keeping the coins was well known and had a good reputation, the receipts were accepted in trade and commerce. In time it became more convenient to have the receipts in different denominations and it wasn't long before they were referred to as "bills." Yet, there was no established currency as recent as the discovered "new world" by Columbus. The first use of paper currency as we know it today appears to have started during the Napoleonic wars in the late 1700s and early 1800s.

Nearly a century before the American Revolution, the colonies attempted to make use of paper money. A. Burton Hepburn reports that in 1690 Massachusetts issued the first paper money printed in America. During the period prior to the end of the French and Indian wars when England gained control of Canada, several colonies issued paper money to help finance the war and other government functions. Some of this currency was backed by coins or other valuables; however, much of it was not and had only the backing of the government of the colony.

As a result, the acceptance of currency was questionable. If there was confidence in the government, the currency was accepted. If not, it was heavily discounted or refused altogether. Most of it depreciated rapidly and more was issued to redeem the earlier issue. In an effort to make the currency acceptable, laws were passed making it "legal tender" and severe penalties were imposed on those refusing to accept it. At first the penalties were rather mild, such as fines or short imprisonments. When these did not bring about acceptance, harsher penalties were imposed, even to make the offender a "non citizen."

Counterfeiting was rampant. In 1726 Pennsylvania issued currency that was well-accepted but the very excellence of the currency invited counterfeiting despite the penalties of "loss of both ears, a fine of 100 pounds and payment of double the loss sustained by anyone suffering because of the counterfeits." In some colonies, the penalty for counterfeiting was death. But that didn't stop the counterfeiting — profits were too great, and the difficulty of enforcing the law made conviction almost impossible. Inflation was so great that in 1763 the English Parliament enacted a law "to prevent paper bills of credit, hereafter to be issued in any of His Majesty's colonies or plantations in America, from being declared legal tender in payment of money, and to prevent the legal tender of such bills as are now subsisting from being prolonged beyond the periods for calling in and sinking the same."

Continental Currency

The Declaration of Independence on July 4, 1776, was a bold step for the struggling colonies. Not only did it defy the greatest military power of the day but it launched the colonies on a political and economic journey that was without precedent. Lacking any significant amount of coin or other hard goods, the Continental Congress resorted to the only alternative available for the financing of the war and that was the issuance of paper currency. The colonies had no factory to produce goods for export, no means of manufacturing arms or ammunition, and no credit abroad. Moreover, the ports were blockaded by the British Navy. On May 10, 1775, even before the Declaration of Independence, but as the war against the British had begun, the Continental Congress authorized an issue of currency and made it legal tender. All of the colonies followed by making this "Continental" currency legal tender. Hoping to stem the tide of depreciation and lack of acceptance of the new currency, on January 11, 1776, Congress passed the following resolution:

> ... any person who shall hereafter be so lost to all virtue and regard for his country, as to refuse to receive said bills in payment, or obstruct or discourage the currency or circulation thereof, and shall be duly convicted by the committee of the city, county, or district, or in case of appeal from their decision, by the assembly, convention, council or committee of safety of the colony where he shall reside, such person shall be deemed, published and treated as an enemy of his country and precluded from all trade or intercourse with the inhabitants of these Colonies.

This didn't stop depreciation of the currency and it became necessary to issue more and more bills. Congress appealed to the colonies to make the bills legal tender and to call in their own bills. This neither stopped counterfeiting nor assured acceptance of the bills. On November 2, 1776, Congress authorized a lottery as a means of raising money, but it failed; no one wanted to pay coin for a chance of winning Continental currency. More than $357 million was issued by the Continental Congress, and this was later to be known as "old tenor" money. In 1780–1781 "new tenor emissions" of $2,070,485 were placed in circulation. These notes were issued by the individual states and guaranteed by the Congress with an imprint on the back. In May 1781, Congress caused the Continental bills to be refunded. At this time, the country had three kinds of currency: (1) notes issued by the Congress called "old tenor," (2) notes issued by the states; and (3) notes issued by the states and Congress called "new tenor" notes. Every attempt to make this money circulate at par failed. The threat of fines, imprisonment, loss of ears and being outlawed did not make people accept the money that had no backing. The attempt by a government to impart intrinsic value to a product that had none in the commercial world failed as it always has and always will.

From the perspective of the late 1900s, it is hard to imagine the fragile nature of the struggling colonies as they attempted to bring about order and confidence in their battle for independence and the formation of a new nation. The United States dollar has been for several decades the accepted currency of the world. We trade with our paper money as though it were gold, and it is used as a measure of value around the world. Not so in the days of the Continental Congress and the fight to be free of the control of the British. Not only did the colonies lack the means to fight — guns, ammunitions, ships, etc. —

but there was no satisfactory means of paying the soldiers or for the material needed. The aid of France, including soldiers, ships, material goods, the all-important granting of credit and spending of "hard" money in support of its army in the states gave the necessary edge to the struggle. In 1781, following the most difficult winter when Washington's soldiers had not been paid in more than a year, French money enabled Washington to pay his men and to move forward to the battle with Cornwallis at Yorktown and the resulting victory that marked the end of the War of Independence.

Once the war against the British was won, the common cause that held the thirteen colonies together was no longer present. They now became thirteen separate groups each with its own ideas of how the new country should be run, and did not have a great deal of understanding of the need for working together. A huge debt and a depreciated currency presented a challenge to the strongest of leaders. Throughout the struggle between the states as they gradually hammered out a constitution and resolved, at least for the time, the issue of "states rights," was the problem of a stable currency. The lessons of depreciation of currency and the futility of attempting to give value to currency by government edict that were experienced during the days of the Continental Congress and the separate colonies were not lost on the framers of the Constitution.

As a result, in 1781 Congress established the Bank of North America, the first to be incorporated in the country. It had a capital of $400,000, its charter was perpetual, and a number of states granted it a charter. In 1784, the Bank of New York, New York City, and the Massachusetts Bank, Boston, were organized. Alexander Hamilton was a controlling influence in the Bank of New York and drew its charter. These banks issued currency that was backed by the resources of the banks and it was readily accepted and circulated at par. It gave the new nation its first stable currency and was an enormous aid to giving business the ability to operate efficiently and with confidence.

The newly framed United States Constitution took note of the difficulties of issuing currency and included in Article I the following: "The Congress shall have power . . . to borrow money on the credit of the United States . . . to coin money, regulate the value thereof, and of foreign coin." Also, "No state shall . . . coin money, emit bills of credit, make anything but gold and silver coin a tender in payment of debts, pass any . . . law impairing the obligation of contracts."

This wording suggests at least that the framers of the Constitution intended that Congress not have the power to issue paper currency with legal tender attributes. Subsequent action in the 200-plus years since has seen Congress take such action (i.e., United States notes, silver certificates, etc.). This point has been the subject of discussion many times but the records of the Constitutional Convention are reasonably clear that the intent was to prohibit such action. The original draft included the words to "emit bills of credit," which would of course have given specific authority to issue currency. In the debate Gouverneur Morris from New York remarked that "if the United States have credit, such bills will be unnecessary; if they have not, will be unjust and useless." Oliver Ellsworth, from Connecticut, strongly supported this position saying it would "shut and bar the doors against paper money." James Wilson, a lawyer from Pennsylvania, felt it would "remove the possibility of paper money," and James Langsdon, representing New Hampshire, preferred omitting the whole plan rather than the three words "and emit bills."

James Madison, delegate from Virginia, was reluctant to strike the words but finally consented when he was satisfied that it would not prevent the government from using credit. The words were stricken out by a vote of four to one. Thus, it is clear that the intent of the Convention was to prohibit the issuing of paper money by the federal government.

From this point on the issuing of paper currency by banks became an accepted means of providing a medium of exchange and a measure and store of value. Establishment of the Bank of the United States on February 25, 1791, despite objections of Jefferson and Madison but with the strong support of Hamilton, who drafted the bill, was the beginning of a long list of banks issuing paper currency. The notes were backed in most cases by specie and were redeemable in gold or silver. This fact caused them to be accepted at par and to circulate freely. In arguing for the bill to create the Bank of the United States, Hamilton went to great lengths to show why it was needed and why it would be superior to other alternatives. His statements seem overly simple to the student of banking today but they set the stage and the premise for today's banking system. It would not serve our purposes to quote extensively from Hamilton's statement but one paragraph seems useful to our discussion of money:

> Among other material differences between a paper currency issued by the mere authority of government and one issued by a bank, payable in coin, is this, that in the first case there is no standard to which an appeal can be made as to the quantity which will only satisfy or which will surcharge the circulation; in the last that standard results from the demand. If more should be issued than is necessary it will return upon the bank. Its emissions, as elsewhere intimated, must always be in a compound ratio to the fund and the demand, whence it is evident that there is a limitation in the nature of the thing; while the discretion of the government is the only measure of the extent of the emissions by its own authority.

Pre-Federal Reserve System Currencies

For convenience in following the story of specific issues of currency in the United States, it seems appropriate to discuss each one separately. This will involve some duplication of statements and ideas already mentioned but will make it easier to trace the issue and use of each currency. We have already talked about efforts of the colonies to print and circulate paper currency.

Confronted by the huge expenses of the American Revolution and without the power of taxation, the Continental Congress on May 10, 1775, authorized the first issue of paper money which went into circulation in August of 1776. This currency, limited to $2 million, was to finance army payrolls and purchase military supplies. Soon, however, several other issues were put out and the total in circulation greatly exceeded all reasonable needs. Because the currency was not backed by gold or silver and because there was extensive counterfeiting by the British, it was soon nearly worthless. George Washington, in commenting on the currency, said, "A wagon-load of money will scarcely purchase a wagon-load of provisions." The highly depreciated value of this currency authorized by the Continental Congress and last issued in 1781 led to the term for worthlessness that has remained to this day — "not worth a continental." Alexander Hamilton, well aware of the dangers of losing all confidence in the fledgling government, led a group that insisted that some kind of redemption be made of these outstanding continental notes. After much debate, in 1790, Congress authorized the Treasury to accept the Continental notes at a rate of 100 to 1 in payment of bonds of the new federal government. The United States government issued no paper currency between 1790 and the Civil War. On several occasions (1812–1815, 1837–1843, 1846–1847, 1857, and 1860–1861) the Treasury issued small amounts of notes, almost always interest-bearing, in denominations ranging down to $50. Some of these notes may have had some circulation, and if so, in very limited amounts, but they were not intended to serve as currency.

From 1791 to 1836, the larger part of paper currency in circulation consisted of issues of the First (1791–1811) and the Second (1816–1836) Bank of the United States, a *private* federally chartered bank. At the time of its closing in 1836, the Second Bank of the United States had outstanding note liabilities of $23,100,000. Because these notes were so readily acceptable, the unreliable paper currency issued by the state banks during the existence of the Bank of the United States was substantially reduced.

A discussion of the Bank of the United States and its issuing of currency would not be complete without looking at the basic and sometimes highly emotional struggle between the proponents of a strong central government and those insisting on the support of "states rights." These two viewpoints were not always expressed in these terms, but underlying much of the debate about a Bank of the United States were firm convictions that any hint of centralizing power was contrary to the intent of the framers of the Constitution and likely to lead to control by a central power against which the very fight for independence was waged. Alexander Hamilton and Thomas Jefferson were the dominant leaders in the debate. Hamilton held out for a strong central government, saying it was critical to the nation's welfare; Jefferson expressed the fear that such centralized power would be disastrous to the nation.

The bill creating the First Bank of the United States was signed into law by President Washington on February 25, 1791, despite the strong objections of Jefferson and others of the same view. At issue was not only the question of a strong central government *vs.* more "states rights," but also a larger question of interpretation of the Constitution. Hamilton argued that the power of Congress to create corporations (and thus a bank) was implied, and that such power was equally authoritative with specific powers outlined in the Constitution. On the other hand, Jefferson and his followers held out for a strict interpretation of the wording of the Constitution, which plainly did not grant such powers. For the next 200 years sincere men would debate this issue with the interpretations shifting inexorably toward the use of implied powers.

The charter of the First Bank of the United States was for a period of twenty years. And in 1811 when a bill to renew its charter came to a vote, the House of Representatives rejected it by a vote of sixty-five to sixty-four. In the Senate the vote against was eighteen to seventeen, with Vice President George Clinton casting the deciding vote. Chaos broke out when the remaining state banks were unable to assist the government in financing the War of 1812. In March of 1816, the House passed a bill creating the Second Bank of the United States by a vote of eighty to twenty-one and the Senate voted its approval on April 10, 1816. The bank opened its doors for business on January 17, 1817, and again the circulation of currency was established.

Unfortunately, the operation of the Second Bank of the United States was plagued with mismanagement, speculation and "insider" transactions. However, by 1820, corrections were made and the Bank served a useful purpose. Action to renew the charter of the Second Bank of the United States, which again was for twenty years, brought on a deluge of opposition and political infighting. As a result, its charter expired and the next twenty-five years were a period of great instability in the nation's currency.

Underneath the debate on the need for and the constitutionality of a central bank was the division among leaders—and the people—over the issue of slavery. This issue remained unresolved until the Civil War ended in 1865.

After the closing of the Bank of the United States in 1836, and until 1861, notes issued by state-chartered private banks were the chief form of paper currency. The states were prohibited by the United States Constitution from issuing currency or coin, but there was no prohibition against private state-chartered banks issuing their own paper notes, often with little backing or supervision.

These state bank notes had varying degrees of acceptability, were not always redeemable in gold or silver on demand, and the issue of many banks frequently circulated at a substantial discount from face value. Each bank chose its own design for its notes and they differed in size, color, and appearance. Because of no effective regulations or controls, some of the banks were insolvent from the beginning. Others, called "wildcat banks" were opened in mountainous and other inaccessible regions where they were difficult to find by persons wanting to redeem their notes. They were called "wildcat" because it would take a wildcat to locate the banks.

By 1860, it is estimated there were notes of 8,000 banks in circulation. Under these circumstances, counterfeiting flourished as never before, bank failures were common throughout the period causing some notes to be called "broken bank notes," and people regularly suffered losses on notes they received and held.

Severe financial panic occurred, and the country was just beginning to recover from the severe panic of 1857 when the Civil War began. That war prompted the passage of the National Bank Act of 1863, authorizing the chartering of national banks with power to issue paper currency notes under prescribed conditions, including the deposit of certain government bonds with the United States Treasurer as collateral. An amendment to the National Bank Act in 1864 placed a prohibitive tax on state bank notes, causing state banks to discontinue their issuance. Thus ended the era of state bank notes.

It could be said that the economy of the United States struggled through that hectic period from 1836 to 1861, not because of help from state bank currency, but in spite of it. It is only fair to say, however, that there were many reliable banks that carefully maintained a required reserve of gold and silver to back their notes.

The first paper money actually issued by the government of the United States consisted of noninterest-bearing treasury notes authorized by Congress on July 17, 1861. These notes, issued in denominations of $5, $10, and $20, were "Payable to Bearer on Demand" in coin at certain designated subtreasuries, and soon became known as demand notes. The notes were issued to help finance the Civil War and to put more money into circulation since people were hoarding their metal money. The amount first authorized was $50 million, but a second issue of $10 million was also paid out. The backs of these notes were green and they soon became known as "greenbacks." It subsequently developed that these notes had no backing other than faith in the government.

Under the Legal Tender acts of 1862 and 1863, Congress provided for the issuance of United States notes and they were substituted for the demand notes, which were retired. The United States notes were first issued in March of 1862 in the amount of $150 million and were designated as legal tender for all debts, except duties on imports and interest on the public debt. They were popularly referred to as "legal tenders." The first issue, "payable to the bearer in _____ dollars at the Treasury of the United States in New York" was in denominations of $5, $10, $20, $50, $100, $500, and $1,000. A second issue of $150 million was also authorized in 1862, and a third issue in the same amount in 1863, which included denominations of $1 and $2. Other issues followed. The highest amount outstanding at any one time was $449,338,902 in early 1864. By 1878, the amount outstanding had been reduced to $346,681,016 and since that date the amount outstanding was always maintained to at least that figure, mostly in denominations of $2 and $5.

It was during the Civil War (January 3, 1862) that the federal government was compelled to suspend specie payment—that is, drop the provision for redeeming the United States notes in coin, and it was not until January 1, 1879, that specie payments were resumed. During this period these "legal tender" notes likewise had no backing other than the "full faith and credit" of the United States, but by law they had to be accepted. The only denomination of United States notes issued today is the $100 bill.

The South had its share of problems with paper currency, also. An early issue was actually printed by an engraving and printing firm in New York City. Some of these notes made it to the Confederacy, while the remainder were confiscated.

Following the suspension of the specie payments by the federal government on January 3, 1862, subsidiary silver coins largely disappeared from circulation: as always happens, bad money sends good money to the hoarders. For a time their place was taken by tickets, due bills, and other forms of private obligations, issued by merchants and others whose business required them to make change. Congress then authorized the use of postage stamps for change (after people had begun to use them for this purpose), and later issued a modified stamp called postal currency. Finally, fractional paper currency was issued in denominations corresponding to the silver coins. Congress authorized an issue of $50 million; the highest amount outstanding at any one time was $49,102,660.27. These "paper coins," much smaller in size than our present currency, were known as "shinplasters" and were issued in denominations of 3-, 5-, 10-, 15-, 25-, and 50-cents. After the end of the war when coinage was resumed this fractional currency was no longer needed, and in 1875 and 1876 Congress provided for its redemption and retirement.

Between the Civil War and the First World War, most of the paper currency in circulation consisted of national bank notes. This currency was issued by banks chartered under the National Bank acts of 1863 and 1864, which required these banks to deliver to the Treasurer of the United States a specified amount (based on their capitalization) of registered United States Treasury bonds bearing the "circulation privilege." The banks were then entitled to receive from the Comptroller of the Currency paper money equal to 90 percent of the value of the bonds. Originally, the total amount of currency for all banks was limited to $300 million. In 1870, it was increased, and in 1875 the limitation was removed. By 1913, national bank notes amounting to almost $700 million were in circulation. The notes were in denominations of $1, $2, $5, $10, $20, $50, $100, $500, and $1,000. All such currency was United States money (national currency) in every respect. National bank notes were uniform in size and general appearance, bore the name and location of the issuing bank, and the signatures of the cashier and president on the face. The last of the bonds having the circulation privilege matured in 1935, and national bank notes have since been retired from circulation.

For awhile after the passage of the National Bank Act, no national banks existed in California. Although the early settlers of the West disliked paper money, they needed it to replace the cumbersome handling of large amounts of gold, silver and metal coins in consummating transactions. On July 12, 1870, Congress extended the National Bank Act to authorize gold banks in California. Nine such banks in California and one in Boston were granted charters similar to those granted to other national banks, which meant that their note issues had to be covered by United States bonds deposited with the United States Treasurer. However, the gold redemption of their notes rested upon the issuing bank and not upon the treasurer.

In 1878 the Treasury was authorized to issue silver certificates. There were five issues of these notes that were authorized by the acts of February 28, 1878, and August 4, 1886. The first issue was in denominations of $10, $20, $50, $100, $500, and $1,000. A second issue in 1886 included $1, $2, and $5 notes. Silver certificates were given out in return for the deposit of silver dollars which were held for their redemption. Later issues were also backed by silver bullion. They have not been paid out since 1964 and in 1968 the Treasurer discontinued redemption. Like other discontinued issues of currency, when outstanding silver certificates are received at a Federal Reserve Bank or branch, they are cancelled and destroyed.

Between 1865 and 1928, there were nine issues of gold certificates, some of which circulated in very limited amounts as they were not intended for general circulation but were used mostly for inter-bank transactions. These notes were issued against gold coins deposited with the treasurer and held for their redemption. The first gold certificates for general circulation were authorized by the act of July 12, 1882. The last issue was in 1928, and they continued in circulation until 1933, after which it became illegal for private citizens to hold them. This ban was lifted in 1964, but they no longer circulated and were held only as collector's items.

"Treasury Notes of the United States" were authorized in 1890. These notes, usually called "Treasury Notes of 1890" or "Coin Notes" because they were redeemable on demand in either gold or silver coin at the discretion of the Secretary of the Treasury, were legal tender. There were only two issues, one in 1890 and one in 1891. The authority for these notes was repealed in 1893, when almost $156 million were outstanding. Congress later provided for the cancellation and retirement of this issue.

Federal Reserve Bank Notes

The Federal Reserve Act of 1913 authorized the issuance of Federal Reserve Bank notes against the deposit of United States bonds. These notes were, in effect, very much like the national bank notes and carried the legend "National Currency." The first issue (Series of 1915) was in denominations of $5, $10, and $20 notes. A second issue (Series of 1918) was in denominations of $1, $2, $5, $10, $20, and $50 notes. In the banking emergency of 1933 and

1934, Congress once again authorized the issuance of Federal Reserve Bank notes secured by direct obligations of the United States or by eligible commercial paper. By the end of 1933, the value of these notes in circulation reached a peak of $208 million. They were retired over the next two years. During World War II a stock of unused Federal Reserve Bank notes was issued in order to save paper and labor that would have been used to produce other needed currency. Following the war, the notes were gradually retired.

Almost all of the paper currency in circulation today consists of Federal Reserve notes, issued under authority of the Federal Reserve Act of 1913, by the twelve Federal Reserve banks. These notes are obligations of the United States and are first liens on all the assets of the issuing Federal Reserve Bank. When issued, Federal Reserve notes are fully backed by collateral which may consist of gold certificates, government securities, or high-grade, short-term commercial paper. The first issue (Series of 1914) was in denominations of $5, $10, $20, $50 and $100 notes. The second issue (Series of 1918) included $500, $1,000, $5,000 and $10,000 denominations. The largest denomination currently issued is the $100 note.

The original Federal Reserve Act provided for redemption of Federal Reserve notes in gold at the United States Treasury or of lawful money at a Federal Reserve Bank. The Gold Reserve Act of 1934 provided that the Federal Reserve notes be redeemable only in lawful money, and since 1933 they have been full legal tender for all debts, public and private.

The printing of the notes in denominations of $500 and larger was discontinued by action of the Board of Governors of the Federal Reserve System on December 27, 1945, because of insufficient demand for them and to discourage their use in business to avoid income tax. Federal Reserve banks continued to issue remaining supplies of these large denomination notes, however, until 1969, when their issuance was finally terminated.

The Saga of the $2 Bill

The $2 bill has had a long and illustrious history. It has been cursed, blessed and touted as a solution to the high cost of printing currency. Viewed as a symbol of bad luck it is shunned at all costs by some. Chambers of commerce have asked for it to celebrate special events in their community. Business firms have asked to use them for their payroll to demonstrate the impact of the company on the economy of the area. Superstitious persons tear off a corner of the bill if it comes into their possession, as this is supposed to break the spell of misfortune attributed to the $2 bill.

This misfit in our system of decimal money was first printed in 1776. Authorized by the Continental Congress as "bills of credit for the defense of America," it was supposed to help finance the War of Independence. Only 49,000 pieces were circulated and then not for long, as they fell under the same discredit as other paper money of the time. During the War Between the States, Congress again authorized the printing of $2 bills. In subsequent years it appeared as United States notes, silver certificates, treasury notes, national bank currency, and Federal Reserve notes. Various portraits were used on the bills, including Alexander Hamilton, James B. McPherson, Winfield S. Hancock, William Windom and George Washington. In 1928 the bill appeared in the new (and current) size with the portrait of Thomas Jefferson. (Until July 1929, our currency was 7.42 inches by 3.13 inches. Since July 1929 it has been 6.14 inches by 2.61 inches—a more convenient size.)

In May 1965, the bill was printed as the series of 1963–1964. Again, the portrait of Thomas Jefferson was used and the bills bore the signature of Secretary of the Treasury Henry Fowler and Treasurer of the United States Kathryn O'Hay Granahan. This time the public practically ignored the bill and it was soon discontinued. It remained for the celebration of the nation's bicentennial to bring the bill back into existence. The American Revolution Bicentennial Administration, Congress, the general public, the Federal Reserve System and collectors all expressed interest in a new $2 bill. Responding to this revival of interest the Secretary of the Treasury authorized the printing of the bill stating that it would be in the best interest of the American public and the economy.

The new bill would continue to use the portrait of Thomas Jefferson on the face of the bill. It would be signed by the then Secretary of the Treasury William E. Simon and Treasurer of the United States Francine I. Neff. On April 13, 1976, the anniversary of Thomas Jefferson's 200th birthday, 225,000,000 new bills were available at Federal Reserve banks. An annual printing of 400,000,000 was anticipated. The face of the bill was similar in design to the 1963 version but the back depicted a rendering by John Trumbull of the signing of the Declaration of Independence. This vignette, based on Trumbull's painting *The Signing of the Declaration of Independence,* was altered from the original to conform to the space available on the bill. The six figures appearing on the extreme left- and right-hand borders of the original art were dropped.

This somewhat sentimental reason for resurrecting the $2 bill as a part of the bicentennial celebration in 1976 is tainted by the purely economic reason of saving money. It was reasoned that if the public would use the $2 bill in place of two $1 bills, it would save printing costs of $35 million over a five-year period. At that time about 1.7 billion $1 bills were being printed annually, accounting for nearly 60 percent of all currency printed. If the public used the $2 bill whenever possible it would reduce by nearly half the need for $1 bills. Such optimism was short-lived; the public looked upon the $2 bill as it had for decades—it didn't like it. Superstition, confusion with the one-dollar bill, unfamiliarity and just plain resistance to change doomed the effort to failure almost before the first bills appeared. Banks ordered them but soon returned them to their Federal Reserve Bank, sometimes without even breaking the seal on the package. By the end of the first year the bills had practically disappeared from circulation. Collectors stored a few as the fact that they were part of the bicentennial celebration gave them some collector's value. Interestingly, the Treasury devoted considerable effort to point out that the bills would be printed in sufficient numbers so that they would not become a collector's item.

In 1983 the Treasury reported fewer than 350,000,000 $2 bills in circulation, and more than 3.5 billion $1 bills in the hands of banks and the public.

Design Characteristics and Symbolism

This seems to be a good place to take a close look at a piece of our currency and see what designer's secrets we can unravel. To begin, the paper used is a very high-quality paper. It withstands much handling by the greasy hands of mechanics, the steady hands of a waitress as well as its crumbling by a boy as he stuffs a bill into the pocket of his blue jeans.

The bill actually consists of two pieces of paper, firmly stuck together with a random assortment of colored threads between them. On the "face" (or front, which is darker green and the side with the portrait) are many items, each with a special meaning. The first item that we usually see is the portrait.

The men portrayed on paper currency are alike in two ways: they were distinguished American statesmen and they are deceased. By law no living person can be portrayed on a bill or any other obligation of the United States. The reason for this legislation goes back to the Civil War when what is known as the Clark incident occurred. Spencer M. Clark, the chief clerk of the National Currency Division of the U.S. Treasury, which later became the Bureau of Engraving and Printing, used his own portrait on 500,000 five-cent notes (fractional currency) issued at that time, causing a stir of disapproval in Congress. Representative M. Russell Thayer of Pennsylvania denounced portraying living persons on currency. He also questioned the use of portraits of persons "not associated with the historic glories of the country." A law was passed by Congress which specifies that "No portrait shall be placed upon any of the bonds, securities, notes, fractional or postal currency of the United States, while the original of such portrait is living" (31 U.S.C. 413). Accordingly, the portraits used on our paper money are those of deceased persons whose places in history are well known to the American people.

Also on the face is the seal of the Federal Reserve Bank that issued the bill. It is to the left of the portrait. The letter in the center of the seal and the number (1 through 12) indicates the bank of issue (A-1 = Boston, B-2 = New York, C-3 = Philadelphia, D-4 = Cleveland, E-5 = Richmond, F-6 = Atlanta, G-7 = Chicago, H-8 = St. Louis, I-9 = Minneapolis, J-10 = Kansas City, K-11 = Dallas, and L-12 = San Francisco).

The Federal Reserve Bank number is repeated in the upper and lower left and right corners of the bill. These numbers are helpful in cases involving

Seal of the Department of the Treasury, which is imprinted upon the face of United States paper money. (Courtesy of the United States Treasury Department.)

claims made by the public for redemption of burned or mutilated notes, when only portions of the notes can be identified.

The original seal of the Department of the Treasury, imprinted upon the face of paper money, is older than the Constitution of the United States. That seal was designed under the direction of a committee appointed September 26, 1778, and composed of John Witherspoon, Gouverneur Morris, and Richard Henry Lee. The date of the original seal's adoption is not known, but the seal is affixed to documents issued as early as 1782.

The new seal of the Department of the Treasury, approved on January 29, 1968, is overprinted on the face of each note to the right of the portrait. This seal has the inscription "The Department of the Treasury," which replaces the former Latin legend *Theasaur. Amer. Septent. Sigil.,* an abbreviation said to represent *Theasauri Americae Septentrionalis Sigillum,* translated as "The Seal of the Treasury of North America." The new seal bears the date "1789," the year of the Department's creation. The balance scales represent justice; the key is the emblem of official authority; and the chevron with thirteen stars for the original states appears on the seal. On United States notes, the Treasury seal, along with the serial numbers, is overprinted in red; on Federal Reserve notes, these features are overprinted in green.

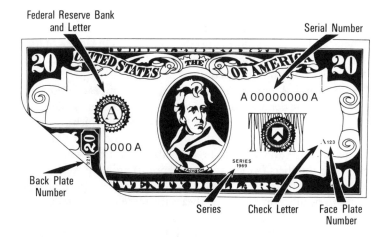

Federal Reserve Bank and Letter

Serial Number

A 00000000 A

Back Plate Number

)000 A

SERIES 1969

Series   Check Letter   Face Plate Number

Face of the $20 Federal Reserve note. (Courtesy of United States Secret Service.)

Also on the face are two identical series of numbers, known as serial numbers, including the prefix and suffix letters, in the upper right and lower left sections of United States currency. Serial numbers on all currency now in common use are always in eight digits. They also have a prefix letter and a suffix letter, unless they are "star" notes. The letters are considered a part of the number. On United States notes, the first note in a new series will have the serial number A 00000001 A, and the second A 00000002 A, and so on.

On Federal Reserve notes, the prefix letter in front of the serial number corresponds to that in the Federal Reserve Bank seal. Notes issued by the Federal Reserve Bank of Dallas are Eleventh District Notes and the letter preceding the serial number is the eleventh letter of the alphabet—K. The notes are numbered in lots of 100,000,000. (Because of the limitation of the numbering system to eight numerals, a "star" note is substituted for the 100,000,000th note.) Each such unit carries a distinctive suffix letter beginning with A and following in alphabetical order through Z, omitting only O because of its similarity to the numeral zero. For example, the serial number of the first run of any denomination note of each series for the Dallas Federal Reserve Bank will carry the letter combination K-A; the second K-B; and so forth through K-Z. The letter in the Federal Reserve Bank seal and the prefix letter of the serial numbers are always indentical; for example, on Federal Reserve Bank of Dallas notes the letter K is in the seal and is the prefix letter in the serial number.

People are sometimes curious about the significance of the star that appears in front of the serial number on some pieces of United States currency.

When a note is mutilated in the course of manufacturing, it has to be replaced. To replace it with a note of exactly the same serial number as that on the imperfect specimen would require the use of special machinery and would be costly and delaying. In consequence, "star" notes are substituted. Except that they have their own serial number with a star, these notes are the same as the others, and of course, worth only the face value. On United States notes, a red star is substituted for the prefix letter; on Federal Reserve notes, a green star is substituted for the suffix letter.

The small capital letter and the number which appear in the upper left corner just below the denomination counter on the face of a bill designates the position of the note on the 32-subject face plate from which it was printed.

The small number of digits in the lower right corner on the face and back of the note indicates the serial number of the plate from which a note was printed. These numbers (which are not identical) are used to determine the face and back press plates from which a particular note was printed. The letter preceding this number on the face is always the same as the letter in the upper left corner.

A series identification appears on all of our currency. The series date, found at the right of the portrait near the signature of the Secretary of the Treasury on the face of each bill, shows the year the design of a note was first adopted and used. The series on currency notes does not change each calendar year as it does on coins, but only when there is a major revision in the basic design. Sometimes a minor change is made in the design that does not constitute a new design or require a completely new engraving plate. In such a case, the series year remains the same but a capital letter is added to indicate that the design differs slightly from previous printings of the particular issue. Such a minor change occurs when a new Secretary of the Treasury or Treasurer of the United States is appointed and new signatures are required. The number of minor changes is shown by the appropriate letter of the alphabet. For example, the 1969C $5 Federal Reserve note means that the particular design has been changed slightly on three different occasions.

Both the obverse and the reverse of the Great Seal of the United States, adopted in 1782, are reproduced on the back of the $1 bills. The obverse depicts an American eagle breasted by our national shield. The eagle holds in its right talon an olive branch of thirteen leaves and thirteen berries, symbolic of peace. In the left talon are thirteen arrows signifying the original colonies' fight for liberty. A ribbon flying from the beak of the eagle is inscribed with the Latin motto *E Pluribus Unum,* translated "One out of many," in reference to the unity of the thirteen colonies as one government. Over the eagle's head is a constellation of thirteen five-pointed stars surrounded by a wreath of clouds.

The reverse of the seal depicts a pyramid, with 1776, the year of the Declaration of Independence, with the Roman numerals MDCCLXXVI on its base. The pyramid represents permanence and strength. Its unfinished condition symbolizes that there is still work to be done to form a more perfect government and signifies the expectation that new states would be admitted to the Union. The eye in the triangular glory represents an all-seeing Deity. The

The Great Seal of the United States. Both the obverse (left) and reverse are printed on the back of $1 bills. (Courtesy of the United States Treasury Department.)

words *Annuit coeptis,* translated as "He [God] has favored our undertakings," refer to the many interpositions of Divine Providence in the forming of our government. *Novus Ordo Seclorum,* translated as "A new order of the ages," sighifies a new American era.

Along with the introduction of small-sized currency notes in 1929, uniform back designs were adopted, many of them including vignettes of buildings or monuments or reproductions of paintings closely associated with the persons pictured on the faces of the notes.

Regardless of the type of currency, all those of the same denomination bear the same portrait. The portraits and back designs on United States currency notes now being printed are as follows:

Denomination and Class	Portrait	Back Design
$1 Federal Reserve note	Washington	Great Seal of the United States (obverse and reverse)
$2 Federal Reserve note	Jefferson	The Signing of the Declaration of Independence
$5 Federal Reserve note	Lincoln	Lincoln Memorial
$10 Federal Reserve note	Hamilton	U.S. Treasury Building
$20 Federal Reserve note	Jackson	White House

Denomination and Class	Portrait	Back Design
$50 Federal Reserve note	Grant	U.S. Capitol
$100 Federal Reserve note	Franklin	Independence Hall
$100 United States note	Franklin	Independence Hall

Notes of the $500, $1,000, $5,000 and $10,000 denominations have not been printed for many years and, as they are returned to the Federal Reserve banks, are removed from circulation. The portraits selected for these notes were: McKinley for the $500; Cleveland for the $1,000; Madison for the $5,000; and Chase for the $10,000. The $100,000 denomination gold certificate bearing a portrait of Wilson, issued only to Federal Reserve banks, did not enter into circulation.

United States paper money is printed by the Bureau of Engraving and Printing in Washington, D.C. The selection of designs used on our paper currency, including portraits, is a responsibility of the Secretary of the Treasury, who acts with the advice of responsible officials, such as the director of the Bureau of Engraving and Printing, the Treasurer of the United States, and the Board of Governors of the Federal Reserve System.

When a new currency note is to be issued, designs are discussed by interested government officials and are then submitted to the designers of the Bureau of Engraving and Printing, who prepare models. The final model must be approved by the Secretary of the Treasury. Photographic copies of the approved model are then furnished to the engravers.

The engravers work with the most modern and sophisticated instruments. Separate portions of the design, such as the portrait, the vignette, the ornaments, and the lettering, are hand cut by engravers specially trained in that particular style. To become an engraver, a person must be inherently artistic and exceptionally skilled in that line of endeavor. To become a skilled picture engraver requires ten years' time; to become a skilled letter engraver requires seven years.

Printing and Circulation

Only the highlights of the printing operation and processing of our paper money are given here. Those interested in a more detailed explanation can obtain from the United States Treasury Department, Washington, D.C., publications which give details about dies, engravings, plates, presses, and other facts about the process of printing our currency.

Because of the most rigid accounting, auditing, security, and other controls employed by the Bureau of Engraving and Printing in the manufacturing of United States paper currency, this is one of the most accurate operations in the world. The printing and processing of billions of pieces of currency are handled on the most modern and sophisticated machines in an accurate, expeditious and economical manner. The minimal errors that occur are due to mechanical defects which are promptly detected and corrected (such as detection of an imperfect note, which is promptly replaced by a "star" note).

All United States paper currency is printed on modern high-speed sheet-fed rotary presses by the dry intaglio process, which provides a relatively high degree of dimensional stability in the paper. Special distinctive paper, manufactured by private contractors under strict government specifications, is used for the printing of all notes.

Each plate produces a sheet of thirty-two subjects or notes. The most recently acquired presses accommodate four plates and are capable of printing 8,000 sheets per hour, an increase of approximately 200 per cent over the first rotary presses purchased by the Bureau.

Upon the completion of the basic back and face printings, the thirty-two-note sheets are trimmed to a uniform dimension and the serial numbers, the Treasury seal, and, in the case of Federal Reserve notes, the Federal Reserve Bank designations, are simultaneously overprinted on the face of each note by the typographic process on two-color rotary presses.

A detailed examination to identify imperfect notes for later removal is made of each sheet, after which the sheets, in units of 500, are cut into individual notes. After a final examination for the removal of the imperfect notes and their replacement with "star" notes, the currency is manually steel-banded and wrapped in packages for delivery. Each currency package contains forty bands of 100 notes each and weighs about 8½ pounds. For example, each package contains 4,000 notes (forty bands of 100 notes each) and the values according to denominations are as follows:

Package of One's	$ 4,000
Package of Two's	$ 8,000
Package of Five's	$ 20,000
Package of Ten's	$ 40,000
Package of Twenties	$ 80,000
Package of Fifties	$200,000
Package of Hundreds	$400,000

These packages of money, totalling billions of dollars, are placed under the strictest accountability down to the last dollar, and are stored under the most rigid security awaiting shipment to the Federal Reserve banks and their branches. Until such completed packages of bills are received by the Federal Reserve offices and released into circulation after they are secured by a pledge of collateral, they are not considered to be money, but just printed paper notes ready to be released into circulation.

In addition to the supply of currency kept available to satisfy the current requirements of the Federal Reserve offices, the Federal Reserve Board has stockpiled billions of dollars in currency in what could be called the Fort Knox of paper money. The currency is kept in a heavily guarded, little-known

complex carved into a hillside near Culpepper, Virginia. This huge supply of new bills, believed to be the most kept in any vault in the world, would be used to replenish the nation's money supply in case of a nuclear attack.

The distribution of United States paper currency is made through the Federal Reserve banks and their branches and by the office of the Treasurer of the United States in Washington, D.C.

There are twelve Federal Reserve head offices and twenty-five branches (shown in parentheses) located in the following cities:

District Number

1	Boston
2	New York (Buffalo)
3	Philadelphia
4	Cleveland (Pittsburgh, Cincinnati)
5	Richmond (Baltimore, Charlotte)
6	Atlanta (Nashville, Birmingham, Jacksonville, New Orleans, Miami)
7	Chicago (Detroit)
8	St. Louis (Louisville, Memphis, Little Rock)
9	Minneapolis (Helena)
10	Kansas City (Omaha, Denver, Oklahoma City)
11	Dallas (El Paso, Houston, San Antonio)
12	San Francisco (Seattle, Portland, Salt Lake City, Los Angeles)

The chairman of the board of each head office bank (appointed by the Board of Governors of the Federal Reserve System) also serves as a Federal Reserve agent. Until 1970, his or her duties in the latter capacity included the responsibility of maintaining an adequate supply of *unissued* Federal Reserve notes of all denominations to meet the needs of the economy in that Federal Reserve district. This function was performed under his or her direction by an assistant Federal Reserve agent at the head office banks and by Federal Reserve agents' representatives at the branches. New *unissued* Federal Reserve notes which have been printed for the twelve Federal Reserve districts, were ordered by these persons from the Bureau of Printing and Engraving as needed in their respective offices, and upon receipt, the packages of notes were stored under the most rigid security and controls in multiple-combination vaults. As long as such notes were held *unissued* in such vaults awaiting withdrawal by the Federal Reserve office where they were located, they were not considered to be money—they were just packages of printed paper waiting to enter circulation and become money.

To obtain Federal Reserve notes, a Federal Reserve Bank or branch applied to the Federal Reserve agent who was located at the head office of the particular reserve bank district. In applying for the notes, the reserve bank pledged

Opposite: High-speed rotary intaglio currency printing press used by the Bureau of Engraving and Printing. (Courtesy of United States Treasury Department.)

Top: Steel-banded packages of newly printed Federal Reserve notes received by a Federal Reserve Bank from the Bureau of Engraving and Printing. Bottom: Bags of newly manufactured coin received by a Federal Reserve Bank from a United States Mint and stored pending shipments to commercial banks. Cents are sacked $50 per bag, nickels $200 per bag, and dimes, quarters, half-dollars and dollars $1,000 per bag for each denomination.

Bundles of "Fit Notes" to be stored by a Federal Reserve Bank with thousands of other such bundles totaling millions of dollars pending shipments to commercial banks when they order currency. "Fit Notes" are those that have been in circulation and deposited with a Federal Reserve Bank by a commercial bank but are still in good condition for further circulation. Each bundle contains 1,000 notes.

with the agent the required collateral to fully back the notes, which might consist of gold certificates, government securities, or high-grade, short-term commercial paper. When such collateral had been pledged and the notes delivered to the ordering Federal Reserve office, they became issued Federal Reserve notes ready to be put into circulation . . . they were now money. When a Federal Reserve office accumulated a surplus of Federal Reserve notes of any denomination in excess of its needs, such notes were returned to the Federal Reserve agent and the collateral was then released.

In 1970, this complicated procedure was changed and now new currency is taken directly into the cash balance of the reserve bank and any surplus is held in the accounts of the reserve bank office.

Each Federal Reserve Bank office maintains in vault storage an adequate supply of Federal Reserve notes of all denominations both new and "fit" to meet the needs of commercial banks in the area. ("Fit" notes are those that have been in circulation and deposited with the Federal Reserve Bank by commercial banks but are still in condition for further circulation.)

Due to constant counting, folding, putting in and taking out of purses and wallets, and other handling, paper currency becomes worn and no longer fit for general use. It is then withdrawn from circulation, destroyed, and replaced by new notes. One-dollar bills last about one year and over 2 billion of them are in circulation. Higher denomination bills last longer.

When commercial banks accumulate a surplus of paper currency beyond their normal requirements, they sell such excess to the Federal Reserve Bank serving the territory in which they are located. Commercial banks endeavor to assort and include in the shipments to the Reserve banks currency which is worn, torn, soiled, and unfit for further circulation. Each Federal Reserve Bank issues operating bulletins stating how such currency shipments must be prepared, such as "packages by denomination, face and top up, enclosed in paper straps, each containing 100 notes, with the name of the depositing bank, date, amount, and the number or stamp of the teller counting the package appearing on each strap," etc.

Upon receipt of the shipments from the commercial banks, they are verified at the reserve banks by bill count on specially designed currency counting and sorting machines. As a part of the verification process high-speed machines sort the bills according to denominations and as to "fit" currency (currency that is still in good condition for further circulation according to established standards), and "unfit" currency (currency that is unfit for further circulation according to established standards). The fit currency is placed in vault storage and held, along with new currency, to fill the orders of commercial banks. The unfit currency is shredded and disposed of as trash.

Until the early 1980s this verification process was done by tellers at Federal Reserve banks. Each package of 100 bills was opened, counted, checked for fitness and counterfeits and fed into a machine that counted the number of the bills. Some sorters, as the tellers were called, could do the counting as well and became experts in detecting counterfeits. Long hours of seeing "good money" gave sorters a sense of what might be irregular and thus likely to be counterfeit. The "feel" of the bill was often a giveaway to a counterfeit. The detail of the portrait also gave indications of a fraud. Even though the sorters would sort thousands of bills daily, they were quick to spot counterfeits.

When a counterfeit is found, it is turned over to the Secret Service for further investigation. Along with the bill will go the name of the bank from which it was received and the initial of the teller who handled it in the commercial bank. Not infrequently, the Secret Service representative would visit the bank and ask to speak to the teller. Showing the teller the counterfeit bill he would ask if the teller remembered who presented the bill. Amazingly, the teller many times would reply in the affirmative; usually, there would be something different about the bill. Sometimes he or she could give general description of the person who presented the bill.

Counterfeiters usually work in groups and often are known to the Secret Service. They would pass the bogus bills in a community and quickly move on to other cities. The task of preventing counterfeiting is still with us today. The use of state-of-the-art copying equipment is such that counterfeiters are becoming very good at their illegal craft. In 1985 plans were being made to make changes in the currency that would make it more difficult to imitate. What these changes may be is a well-guarded secret for obvious reasons.

Sometimes a person may inadvertently leave some paper currency in clothing put through a washer. Others may recover portions of bills involved in a fire or salvage portions of a bill or bills that have become mutilated in other ways. Such burned and mutilated currency is exchangeable only by the Treasurer of the United States which affords relief under the following conditions, quoted from Department of the Treasury publication "Facts About United States Money":

> Lawfully held paper currency of the United States which has been mutilated will be exchanged at its face amount if clearly more than one-half of the original whole note remains. Fragments of mutilated currency which are not clearly more than one-half of the original whole note will be exchanged at face value only if the Treasurer of the United States is satisfied that the missing portions have been totally destroyed. This judgment is based on such evidence of total destruction as is deemed necessary and is final. No relief will be granted on account of paper currency of the Unitd States which has been totally destroyed.

It would be advisable for a person who desires to exchange worn, burned or mutilated paper currency to discuss the matter with a commercial banker or with a representative of a Federal Reserve Bank or branch who can advise him what action to take. No method for the restoration of unfit paper currency by washing or other treatment has proven practical. This also would be advisable in disposing of worn and mutilated coin.

Mutilated coins will not be accepted at their face value at Federal Reserve banks or branches or by the Treasurer of the United States but should be shipped to the United States Assay Office, 32 Old Slip, New York, N.Y., 10005 at the expense and risk of the owner (charges prepaid) in accordance with Treasury Department Circular No. 55.

Coins are mutilated when punched, clipped, plugged, fused together, or when so defaced as to be not readily and clearly identifiable as to genuineness and denomination. Coins containing lead, solder, or substances which will render them unsuitable for coinage metal will not be accepted by the mints.

Coins that are bent or twisted out of shape, but are readily and clearly identifiable as to genuineness, and coins that have been reduced in weight by natural abrasion only, are not regarded as mutilated and will be accepted at their face amount.

The Department of the Treasury does not pay a premium for old or rare coins or paper currency. Currency and coin dealers should be contacted regarding the numismatic value of such money. Notes issued by the Confederate states during the Civil War and those issued by the various states or state banks are not redeemable by the Department of the Treasury, and foreign money is neither received nor redeemed by the United States.

The determination of whether material submitted for redemption is actually United States paper currency and the determination of denomination are by direct examinations by specialists with the aid of magnifying glasses and good illumination. The identification of currency from mere fragments, some of which may be completely charred, is one of the unusual jobs in government service. This work requires a thorough knowledge of all United States currency, limitless patience, a delicate touch, and a determination to do a good job. The skilled employees engaged upon this task work with the simplest tools including pins, tweezers, blotters, cotton, strong lights and magnifying glasses.

Thousands of people who send in fragments of currency indicate little hope of getting any return. Much of it would have to be regarded as a total loss but for these painstaking efforts to identify mutilated currency so that the Treasurer of the United States may have a proper and legal basis for redeeming it. The following brief accounts illustrate some of the circumstances having to do with mutilated or burned currency cases that are brought to the Treasurer for redemption:

> When leaving home, a man in North Carolina placed $400 in a small glass jar and hid it in the flue of the kitchen stove. Upon returning from the trip, his first action was to make a roaring fire in the stove. By the time he remembered the currency hidden in the flue, the notes had been severely charred but they were nicely preserved in molten glass and he was able to recover almost the entire amount.

> A farmer in Minnesota buried a strongbox full of currency in the corner of a wheat field. After several years, the $20,000 that he thought the box contained had become fused into a hardened mass. The currency was soaked for days by the skilled examiners to make it soft enough to work on. A total of $27,000 was identified.

> It was rumored in a small West Virginia community that an elderly couple had a fortune buried on their farm. Thieves heard the rumor and ransacked the house. The couple refused to tell where the money was buried, and they were murdered. In order to cover their crime, the killers set fire to the home. The couple's children found $6,000 buried in tin cans under the kitchen floor, and sent the badly burned currency to the Treasury for redemption. The entire amount was refunded to them.

As stated above, no relief will be granted on account of paper currency that has been totally destroyed. When currency is reduced to ashes—that is, light, fragile flakes or powder as distinguished from blackened but solid fragments—identification cannot be made. It is also useless to submit material in the form of pulp or a mass of grains or crumbs. Although currency is made of the best materials, the paper and ink do not leave a residue as ashes, pulp, grains or crumbs that would give information about denominations, or even that the residue resulted from the destruction of genuine currency. However, when some solid fragments remain, it is highly important not to disturb such fragments any more than is absolutely necessary and to properly prepare them for shipment to the Treasurer's office. It would be highly advisable to consult a banker or a representative of a Federal Reserve Bank or branch about this matter.

Chapter Four
Checkbook Money

What Is a Check?

"Do you have money with you?" "Not much, but I have my checkbook."

This conversation is repeated many times as two people — usually husband and wife — embark on a shopping trip. And in most stores the check will be readily accepted. Usually, some identification such as a current driver's license is required. But checks are an accepted means of payment for goods and services in the United States. In recent years the credit card has become of equal importance and we will investigate its development and use in the following chapter.

A check is simply a written order to one party to pay a certain sum to another party. The wording is usually, "Pay to the order of [   ]." Most checks are directed to (we say written on) a bank. The word bank is used in its broadest sense to include savings and loan associations, credit unions and other financial institutions that offer checking services.

In the United States the Negotiable Instruments Act, passed in 1897, spelled out the requirements of a check. It had to be for a sum certain, dated, the amount written in figures and in script, pay to the order of indicated, and signed. Also, it had to carry the name of the party — the bank — to which it is directed. The party to which it is payable is called the "payee." The bank on which it is drawn is called the "drawee" and the party signing the check is called the "maker." In the 1960s adoption of the Uniform Commercial Code, which includes much of the material, including references to checks, found in the Negotiable Instruments Act, became the accepted guide in regard to checks.

Some of the more important rules and regulations governing the handling of checks include: The date on the check cannot be later than the time it is to be paid by the drawee (it cannot be "post dated"); the amount in figures must agree with the written amount but if not, then the written amount governs; the payee must endorse — sign his or her name on the back of the check; each subsequent handler of the check also must endorse it; if the drawee fails to return a check to the previous endorser by midnight of the first business day following receipt, it is considered paid and the drawee does not have any recourse except in the case of fraud, which has no time limitation.

The drawee can refuse to pay a check for many reasons. The most common is that the maker does not have sufficient funds in the account to pay the check—"returned for insufficient funds." Other reasons include lack of endorsement by the payee, no signature by the maker, payment stopped, and "refer to maker." The need for returning a check can delay its final payment several days. With all these rules and possible problems with checks they are still the most frequently used means of payment. The number of checks written in the United States in 1984 was estimated at more than 40 billion and the number continues to increase.

Checks have been written on many kinds of material. Paper is the most often used and the preferred material. It is more easily handled, cheap and adapted to mechanical processing. But it need not be written on paper to be legal. The watermelon growers of Parker County, Texas, once wrote the check in payment for the display of the largest watermelon of the season on a watermelon. It was carried to the bank and marked "paid" and the proper account of the maker charged. Checks have been written on boards to publicize the lumber industry, on large pieces of cardboard to make a presentation more spectacular, on a piece of scrap paper when nothing else was available and on paper with pictures of mountains, rivers, livestock and other objects to give publicity to a place, town or region. As long as the writing contains the essential elements of a check, its payment can be enforced.

The amount of a check can be anything from one cent to millions of dollars. Many of today's mechanical tools for handling checks are programmed to "throw out" checks over a certain amount, such as $1,000,000. It facilitates the operation of the machine not to have provisions for so many digits. And it also calls attention to the large amount and permits special handling if needed.

Thomas Edison, the prolific inventor, is reported to have had a very confusing experience with his first check. According to his biographer, George S. Bryan, the following took place. In about 1870 the president of Western Union, Marshall Lefferts, called the young inventor Edison, who had been working for him, to his office and said "Let's settle this matter of inventions." The latest invention by Edison was an improved teletype machine and Lefferts asked Edison how much he thought it was worth for that and other inventions he had made for Western Union. Edison was almost penniless at the time but thought to himself that it might be worth $5,000. To be safe, he decided in his own mind to ask for only $3,000. But even that seemed too much so he asked Mr. Lefferts to make an offer. That seemed a reasonable request so he replied "How does $40,000 strike you?" Shocked by such a large amount Edison was almost speechless and nearly fainted. Lefferts suggested he think it over.

Three days later Edison came in to sign the contract and collect his money. Payment was, of course, by check. Edison took the check to the bank and

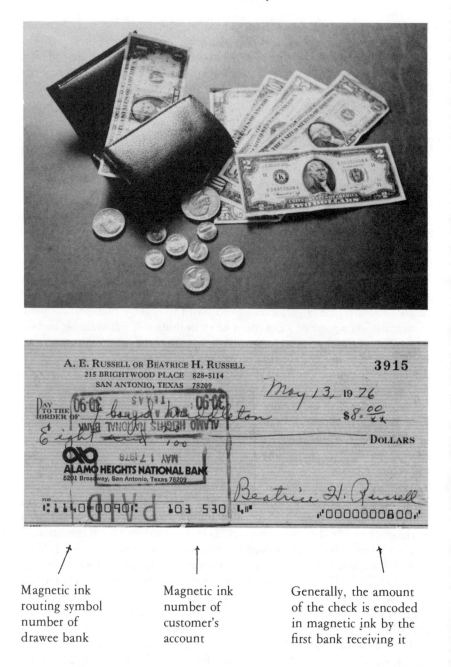

Magnetic ink routing symbol number of drawee bank

Magnetic ink number of customer's account

Generally, the amount of the check is encoded in magnetic ink by the first bank receiving it

Top: "Pocketbook money," or, currency and coin held by the public, comprises less than two percent of the nation's money supply. Bottom: An example of a cancelled check.

passed it to a teller. The teller pushed it back to him to sign. Being hard of hearing, Edison misunderstood and thought the check was not good. He went back to Lefferts and explained his problem. Lefferts, somewhat amused, sent a clerk back with Edison and the teller cashed the check. However, perhaps partly in fun, he paid the check in small bills. Edison stuffed his pockets with the bills and went home. He couldn't sleep that night for fear someone would steal his money. The next day, Lefferts went to the bank with him and helped him open a checking account — his first.

The Development of Checks

The beginning of checks as money is lost in antiquity. As we noted in earlier chapters, the inconvenience of carrying gold or other coins brought about the use of receipts for the deposit of coins and other material of intrinsic value as a substitute for coins. If the reputation of the holder of the valuable and that of the one presenting the receipt were acceptable, it served the role of money. These pieces of paper were first called bills and the term persisted for many years.

Widespread use of a check probably began in England around the middle of the eighteenth century. As the Bank of England was given exclusive power to issue notes or currency, private banks found it increasingly difficult to expand their operations. They soon discovered that they could issue printed checks and thus avoid the need for currency. This new money was readily accepted in trade and industry in England. By issuing credit in the form of a deposit, then giving the depositor (or borrower) the right to write checks against this deposit, the banks found that they could expand their resources without the use of currency. Experience proved that, at any given time, only a portion of the deposits would be withdrawn and they could expand loans in relation to the need to honor the checks.

This ability of commercial banks to create money through loans and deposits is the heart and soul of today's banking industry. It's a very simple operation. The borrower rarely wants his money in cash. He is agreeable to having his account credited and then he will draw against the deposit with a check as funds are needed. Again, so long as everyone doesn't write checks withdrawing all of the deposit at the same time, the bank has no need for currency or coin. Today, most banks carry less than 5 percent of their deposits in cash. This is adequate to meet the needs of their customers.

This new way of creating money used by the banks in England in the eighteenth century was so effective that they forgot all about wanting to issue notes. This new-found source of money has obvious dangers. Without any control by outside parties, the only limit on expansion was the integrity of the bankers and in some cases the imagination of those set on greater and greater expansion. Inflation became a problem and serious laws were enacted to place some

Top: Amount inscribing machine, used by Federal Reserve banks, large commercial banks, and some business organizations, to encode in magnetic ink the dollar amount on checks in the lower right-hand corner. Bottom: A computerized check sorter used by the Federal Reserve banks to process checks. The machine reads the magnetic ink numbers on checks, sorts according to drawee bank, endorses, adds the amounts, and totals at the rate of 100,000 items an hour.

One unit of a computerized system used in a large commercial bank to read the customers' magnetic ink account numbers at the bottom of the checks, sort the checks, reads the amount inscribed in magnetic ink in the lower right hand corner of the checks and make charges to customers' accounts.

limitation on the expansion by the banks. It is not our purpose in this dissertation to bore our readers with the evolution of banking control but let us recognize that with the advent of the check, money took on a whole new dimension. It is estimated that more than 90 percent of all business transactions in the United States are made by check. We will see in the next chapter that "plastic money" threatens to assume a large portion of this business, but the check remains the dominant form of money in the world today.

Prior to the development of machines that could read figures the printed check took many forms and shapes. Each bank attempted to make its checks unique—in effect, a part of its advertising. Checks on banks in the ranch country featured pictures of cattle. Cotton country banks carried the picture of a huge cotton boll. Industrial areas added images to reflect their major business—cars, tractors, steel, etc. Some banks preferred large checks, up to seven or eight inches long, and others gave their customers a choice of small, billfold-style checks or larger "bookstyle" checks.

Check Processing

The advent of machines that could read a code on checks plus the need to process millions of checks on a daily basis stimulated efforts to make all checks a uniform size. It was argued that the machines would be more efficient, but in fact, the early machines could not handle a variety of sizes. The American Bankers Association and the Federal Reserve System in the United States set up study groups to develop some uniform features for the millions of checks moving through the banking system. The problem centered around the need for the check to pass through the machine so that a certain part of the check would always be in a given position. Thus, one of the first ideas was to have uniform checks and place the code for the machine to read on the back of the check. Bank of America initiated this system and pushed for its wide acceptance.

The idea of a uniform-size check failed completely. It was impossible to eliminate the various features in pictures and the size from the checks of 15,000 or more banks. Bank America's idea of placing the amount and drawee bank on the back of the check ran afoul of the practice of placing endorsements on the back of the check—a requirement of law. By the time a check had passed through four or five hands the endorsing stamps in a variety of forms made it impossible to use this area for machine processing.

A second refinement in the sorting machines was the use of magnetically impregnated ink for printing the code on the check. This enabled the machine to read the magnetic characters even though overprinted by endorsements or other printing. The question then arose of where to place the code. Also, should it be in lines or in Arabic figures that could be read by anyone? About this time there was a move to promote a card check with holes punched in it to indicate the amount and other information. The United States Treasury had used this method for several years. The early check-processing machines, usually called sorters, read the punched holes for the amount and the government account to be charged; billions of government checks were processed in this manner. In fact, it was not until the early 1960s that the Treasury moved to the more efficient magnetically encoded check.

As the study groups of the American Bankers Association and the Federal Reserve System struggled to find an acceptable way of encoding checks with the necessary information so that they could be handled by the constantly improving machines, they were bombarded with proposals from bankers, consumers, and the machine manufacturers, each with its own idea of what would work best. It is a credit to the courage of this study group that in 1956 they proposed, and the banking group and the Federal Reserve banks agreed to, a position on the lower edge of the check. The configuration of the magnetic printing was to give the number of the drawee bank, the official routing symbol, the customer's account number and the amount. These figures were to be in Arabic so they could be easily read. With the agreement of the manufacturers of equipment and the check printing industry, promotion was begun to gain acceptance of the program. It was not readily accepted by everyone: customers objected to "those funny figures" at the bottom of their checks, printers objected to the higher cost of using magnetic ink and the quality control that was necessary, and banks found the need to imprint the amount on all checks handled by them to be an increased cost.

But the sheer weight of the growing volume of checks — increasing 8 to 10 percent each year — soon forced compliance with the program. By the late 1970s machines were reading checks at the rate of 1,000 per minute, and computers were at the same time sorting them into various groups and accumulating totals by different categories. In effect, they were doing the work of thousands of workers who would have had to do the work manually. Today, the typical check is imprinted by the printer with magnetic ink showing the number of the drawee bank, routing symbol to show which Federal Reserve district it is in, the customer's account number and in some cases another symbol for use by the bank. As the check is used, the first bank that handles it places the amount of the check in the appropriate place in the line of characters on the bottom of the check, also in magnetic ink. From that point on, machines take over and the check is not manually handled until it is filed in the customer's account file at the drawee bank. There is even a trend towards not filing the check but placing its image on microfilm and providing the customer only with a listing of checks charged to his account. Copies of the checks could be provided on request.

Checkbook money now is by far the most common form of money. Coins and currency are used only when necessary. Carrying large sums of either currency or coin is considered inconvenient and risky. If cash is lost or stolen, there is no recourse.

Advantages and Disadvantages of Check Writing

The check has many advantages. The funds can be directed to a specific person or firm and the writer of the check can be sure that, short of a forged endorsement, the funds will go to the proper person. It can be mailed safely, sent by a third party, or given directly to the party who is entitled to have the money. If lost, payment can be stopped. Once endorsed (signed on the back) by the payee (the one to whom it is written) it can become a negotiable instrument and passed as money. It can be endorsed with a restriction such as "for deposit only" or it can be endorsed to a third party with the words "pay to the order of _____." It can be used as a record of payment to prove an obligation has been discharged or to prove payment to organizations such as charitable groups. Checks can be post-dated, that is, dated at a future time, thus delaying use of the funds.

The use of checks can result in the use of the same money by two or more parties at the same time. For example, a resident of California sends a check to a New York firm in payment of merchandise. It will take from one to three days for the check to reach the party in New York. If he deposits it the next business day (it could be over a weekend or a holiday) his bank will process it, crediting his account and forward it to the drawee bank in California. Depending on the form of transportation used this can take from a day to a week. In the meantime, both the maker and the payee have the use of the funds since the maker's account has not been charged until the check arrives at the drawee bank and the payee in New York has had the use of the funds as soon as it was deposited at his bank. This delay in charging the check creates what the industry calls a "float." The amount of float in the United States on a given day reaches billions of dollars. Any delays in transportation can cause the amount to skyrocket.

The disadvantage of this procedure is that the receiver of the check cannot be certain that the check is valid until it has been finally paid by the drawee bank. If it is not good for any reason, the receiver will not know it until the week or so that it has taken for the check to be processed and the receiver's bank notified that the check is not good.

Double-digit interest rates for overnight money encourages float. During the 1970s and the early 1980s interest rates as high as 20 percent stirred the imagination of money managers in dozens of corporations. Faced with the opportunity of selling any excess funds overnight at a high rate of interest, they looked around for ways to delay the collection of checks issued by them and to speed up the collection of checks given to them in payment of bills. It didn't take long for them to discover that if they had their checks drawn on a bank in a remote area it would take longer for them to clear. For example, a firm in New York that wrote its payroll checks on a local bank would have the bulk of them cleared in one or two days—not much float here. But if the corporation had an account with a bank in the hinterlands of Montana it might take several days, or even a week for them to be cleared and charged to the account of the corporation. In the meantime, the funds could be sold and the high interest earned—a nice way to make money work.

One more wrinkle was to open the account at the remote bank but not keep any large amount on deposit, but have just enough to obtain the services of the bank in clearing the checks. But this meant that when the checks arrived at the remote bank, the corporation must immediately send money to cover them. Wire transfer facilities of "Bankwire" or the "Fed" were available and money could be moved across the country in a matter of minutes. So when the remote bank received the checks from its Federal Reserve Bank it would immediately wire the corporation treasurer and tell him how much money was needed. The corporate treasurer would sell enough of his excess funds to transfer the money to the bank. Everything worked fine as long as the wire facilities worked and the transfer was made at the right time.

This is reminiscent of the circuitous routing of checks during the 1800s. It presents problems to payees of the checks as they cannot be sure the check is good for several days. Also, employees may have difficulty cashing their payroll checks in their hometown as the checks are drawn on a bank that is unknown to the grocery store or other merchant that may be asked to cash the check. It is not an efficient use of checks. But when interest rates are high, the temptation is great to use this device for obtaining float.

Another disadvantage of the use of checks is the possibility of "kiting." This is a fraudulent use of checks done by opening accounts with two or more banks. A check is written on bank A and deposited at bank B. Before it has a chance to reach A for payment, a check is written on bank B to cover the check drawn on bank A. If a third bank is brought into the picture, it can be a three-way process with checks being written on one bank to cover checks on another. By carefully timing the arrival of the checks, it is possible to build up substantial sums and at the critical point in time, withdraw funds in cash and leave the country.

Partly because of this danger in the use of checks, banks are continually striving to speed up the collection. They are also alert to kiting possibilities — if a customer is using more than one bank for checks and the frequency of transactions is considerable, they will take steps to stop the process. A more recent method of moving sums of money between geographic points is by the use of wire facilities. With a network of wire facilities money can be moved from one bank to another or to the account of a third party in a matter of minutes. This method is virtually error-free, and there is no float and no possibility of kiting. More about this method of moving money later.

The Cost of Writing Checks

From the beginning of the use of checks, some financial institutions assessed a charge against the writing of checks in the form of an exchange charge. The charge usually hit the payee of the check first but ultimately the writer of the check absorbed the fee. Tracing the path of a check is the easiest way to illustrate this aspect of checkbook money. Assume that you live in Austin, Texas, and write a check in payment for a car you buy in the neighboring town of Round Rock, Texas, ten miles away. Further, assume that the check is written on your account in an Austin bank. It would seem logical for the payee of the check to deposit the check at his bank in Round Rock and for that bank to send the check down the road to Austin for collection. But in the days prior to the Federal Reserve System, the Round Rock bank might have had an arrangement with a bank in New York to collect all of its checks. One reason for such an arrangement would be that if the check was sent directly to the Austin bank, there would be an exchange charge, sometimes as much as 10 percent of the amount of the check. However, the New York bank, usually in return for a continuing deposit from the Round Rock bank, agreed to pay for all checks sent to it by Round Rock at par — meaning no exchange charge.

The next logical step would be for the New York bank to send the check to the Austin bank for collection, absorbing the exchange charge. But the New York bank might have an arrangement with a bank in Chicago to collect its checks at par. So the check would be sent to Chicago. Now let's hope that the Chicago bank has an arrangement with an Austin bank for collection of checks. But no, it has an arrangement with a bank in Dallas, Texas. So the check goes to Dallas. Now the check is back in Texas and ready to go to Austin, but that Dallas bank does not have a working arrangement with an Austin bank, but it does with one in Houston. Now the check goes to Houston and this bank does have connections with the Austin bank and sends it to the drawee bank for payment. Assuming there are adequate funds in the check-maker's account, the check is paid and the funds reverse the route of the check as each bank in turn remits the amount. The drawee bank will have deducted the service charge but other banks in the chain, by agreement, will send the face amount.

Just to make it more complicated, suppose the maker of the check does not have enough money in his account to pay for the check. So the Austin bank sends it back up the line with a notation of insufficient funds. It will travel the same route in reverse. In all, this may take three or four weeks. So a month after the sale the poor seller of the auto in Round Rock is notified by his bank that the check was not good, and by that time the buyer of the car may be in Mexico and beyond the reach of the seller. But let's assume that the buyer was a longtime customer of the seller and he was sure he could collect from him. He calls him and tells him the sad story. The buyer, embarrassed, quickly apologizes and says, "Let me give you another check." Again, because he is a valued customer, the seller does not want to offend the buyer but he does ask if adequate funds are on deposit at the Austin bank. Assured that they are, he jumps into his car and drives the ten miles to the Austin bank and presents the check "over the counter" and receives his money and does not have any exchange charge for presentation over the counter.

In this illustration, we see that checkbook money is not always money. Circuitous routing of checks and delays in transportation can make a check "potential" money.

With the passage of the Federal Reserve Act in 1913 efforts were undertaken to improve the check-collection process. The act provided for the establishment of check-clearing facilities at each Federal Reserve Bank. The Board of Governors of the Federal Reserve System felt that the development of efficient check-collection arrangements was a high priority. The act specified that checks collected through the Federal Reserve banks be collected at par—with no exchange charge. Inasmuch as the Federal Reserve banks did not charge for the services of check collection, most large banks quickly took advantage of this means of collecting checks. Many smaller banks, especially state-chartered banks, were very reluctant to forego the exchange charges as they were a substantial part of their income. In towns where there was no competition it was easy to maintain the charges. When competition was intense, most banks quickly came to accept the idea of paying all checks at par.

In 1916, the Federal Reserve banks adopted a program of compulsory paying at par and attempted to require all banks receiving checks from the Fed to pay at par. This did not make friends for the Fed banks. In the attempt to force banks to remit at par, Federal Reserve banks sent the checks drawn on nonpar banks by messenger and presented the bundle of checks "over the counter" when they would have to be paid at par. An interesting story is told by an employee of one of the Federal Reserve banks who was sent on such a mission. Upon arrival at the drawee bank, the messenger presented the bundle of checks over the counter and demanded payment. Under the law, the drawee bank could not refuse to pay for the checks but it could take a reasonable time to examine the checks and be certain that the maker had adequate funds on deposit to pay the checks, and also to check to see if they were properly endorsed. This could take all day if the banker was very busy and wanted to delay the Fed's messenger—in effect, expressing his displeasure with the Fed's policy. On this one occasion, the banker told the messenger to have a seat and wait. A few minutes later he tied a dollar bill in a knot and tossed it over the teller's cage and said, "Here's one of them." This went on all day as the banker tied each bill in a knot and tossed it over the teller's cage. This kind of coercion did not work and the Federal Reserve banks soon discontinued this tactic and adopted more subtle plans. Soon, they discontinued sending any checks to a bank that would not pay at par. Thus, a system of collecting them through other commercial banks developed. The practice of charging customers for writing checks continued for years. As late as 1970 a few small remote banks used this method of earning revenue.

Handling checks is an expense to the drawee bank. Most of the time income from the balance in the maker's account does not cover this expense. The charge to recover this cost is now made directly to the customer in the form of a maintenance charge, or in some banks by a flat charge for each check written. This places the cost where it should be—on the user of the checks. An exchange charge penalized the payee of the check and complicated transactions where the charge was not common and generally misunderstood.

The climax to the story of nonpar banks came in 1980. A routine communication from the Board of Governors stated that there was only one nonpar bank remaining in the United States and that was in Louisiana. Noting this, the officer of the Federal Reserve Bank serving that area called the bank and half jokingly said, "You have won the honor of being the only nonpar bank in the United States. When the next list comes out it will show only your bank." The banker replied that he was not sure they wanted that honor and he would take it up with his board of directors. The next day, the Fed officer received a call from the banker saying that as of that date, they would pay all checks at par. Thus ended the 100 or more years of nonpar checks.

It should be understood, as mentioned earlier, that the cost of writing checks is still passed on to the customer but through the use of direct charges to the owner of the checking account. The payee of the check receives the full amount of the check. In the early 1980s concern was expressed by customers and by some members of Congress that banks were charging too much for this service. Also, banks were accused of delaying for an undue length of time the credit for checks deposited with them. This was especially true of government checks. There was some validity to the criticism and the supervisory authorities issued a statement urging all financial institutions to carefully review their operations and policies so that they would not be unduly penalizing customers by delaying credit for checks deposited. The reason for the delay was to be sure that the checks are good. Even though the check-collection system has greatly improved and many times a check sent to New York from California will be cleared the next day after receipt by the payee, delays do occur and banks have on occasion suffered losses when a check is returned for nonpayment. Also, checks issued by the government and transported by the postal service have been stolen from mailboxes and negotiated by forging the endorsement of the payee. Checks issued to persons already deceased have been cashed by kinfolk. The fact that a United States Treasury check is never considered finally paid, that is, the government can go back to the bank and demand reimbursement for a check illegally paid, has made banks unusually cautious in handling these checks. But some became overzealous in using these reasons for delaying credit to depositors.

Electronic Money

This brings us to the next step in checkbook money—electronic money. The technological explosion of the 1960s and 1970s brought many new and improved tools to the banking business. The mechanical handling of paper checks by computers was a giant step forward in handling the mountain of checks, but the advent of electronic transmission of messages opened up an entirely new field. Now customers and banks could transfer money across the country in minutes. Banks had been using telegraph facilities to transfer money between banks for several years, but as electronic equipment became more efficient and computers were linked to the network of transmission wires, moving money from place to place became not only quicker but more accurate. Computers of different banks were now linked to each other and charges and credits were automatically made to accounts.

The forerunner to the widespread use of electronic transfer of funds began with the growth of the market of funds between banks. This is known as the "federal funds" market. The name federal comes from the fact that most of the transfers are made on the books of Federal Reserve banks. Also, the Federal Reserve banks have the most convenient system of transferring money by wire. Since most financial institutions maintain accounts with their Federal Reserve Bank, it is a simple matter to ask the Fed to charge one bank's account at the Fed and credit the receiving bank's account at its Fed bank. Most transfers are for overnight, or until the next banking day. Transactions are usually arranged by telephone and consummated through the Fed's network of wires. Sometimes collateral is pledged by the receiving bank but most often none is involved. But if a bank is slow in returning a transfer the following banking day or even fails to do it, that bank soon is out of the federal funds business. No bank wants to do business with one that does not live up to the understanding of the transaction.

Buying and selling funds does not make much sense unless the philosophy of modern banking is understood. Obviously, banks are in business to make a profit, and to make a profit they must invest the funds deposited with them in loans or securities. On any given day a bank may have funds that it cannot quickly loan to customers or invest in securities. Also, it may be that it anticipates needing the funds within a day or two and does not want to tie them up in a transaction that will not be easily reversed. At the same time other banks may be short of funds to meet the needs of the day; sometimes funds are needed to meet the required reserve balance at the Federal Reserve Bank. At other times, funds may be needed to overcome a sudden withdrawal of deposits that the bank knows is temporary.

Thus, there exists a willing buyer and a willing seller of money — the requirements of a market. Now all that needs to be done is to bring them together and establish a price. In the banking business there are many relationships between banks. Banks maintain balances with each other to facilitate completing various transactions. As with any business, banks have favorite persons with whom they prefer to do business. Let's cite an example and follow a typical federal funds transaction.

Bank A located in rural Oklahoma has an excellent working relationship with a much larger bank in Tulsa. On this particular day the country bank discovers that it has more funds than it can use effectively. A large deposit came in late the previous day and loan demand is slow, but it is also the season of the year when it can soon expect many customers to come in for a loan. So this morning the vice president calls his friend at the bank in Tulsa and offers to sell the Tulsa bank $100,000 overnight. His friend, knowing that he can use the funds, agrees to buy them and to pay 8 percent, to which the country banker agrees. Both bankers make entries on their books reflecting the transaction and the selling bank calls his Fed bank and requests the transfer to the buying bank.

In an hour or two the Tulsa banker has had several calls and now he has a surplus of funds, so he calls his friend in a New York bank and inquires about the market for funds that day. The New York banker already has more than enough funds, but offers 7 percent anyway. Knowing that this is now the market the Tulsa banker agrees. He can't use the funds at his bank overnight and 7 percent is better than nothing. The Tulsa banker will instruct his Fed office in Oklahoma City to charge his account and transmit the funds to the New York Fed. The New York Fed will credit the receiving bank's account and notify it that it has been done.

No pieces of paper have changed hands. The Tulsa bank will confirm its request to the Fed in Oklahoma City, but it will be the next day. It is understood that the New York bank will return the funds the next business day unless instructed to the contrary by the Tulsa bank.

These transactions were further refined in the early 1980s by placing a computer terminal in the country bank—in fact, in most banks—so each bank can initiate transactions in its own office. It will have a printout of the charges and credits, as it can send and receive transfers on its own equipment. The sale or purchase is still arranged by telephone but the mechanics are done by computer. When using the Fed wire system, the accounting will be automatically reflected on the books of the Fed banks involved. Billions of dollars are moved daily through this system. Some are between banks for customers of those banks. A cattle buyer in Texas can instruct his bank to send a sum of money to his associate in Illinois or wherever, using the wire transfer system. The transfer would simply be changed to be "for the credit and advice of [his buyer]."

Extensive and widespread use of wire transfers created a new problem— daylight overdrafts. As a financial institution or corporation participates in the active and sensitive market for funds, it may sell more funds than it has in its account with the Fed. It anticipates ending the day with its account adequate, but if sending institutions fail to transfer promptly or if technical difficulties slow or stop the transfers, it could end the day with an overdraft. At any given time during the day a financial institution can be overdrawn at the Fed, or in the case of a corporation, at its bank. Thus, during the "daylight" it would be overdrawn.

Because of the danger of problems arising through delays or, at the extreme, a failure of a bank or corporation, the Fed could be left holding the bag. In early 1986, the Fed requested that financial institutions make provisions to avoid daylight overdrafts. Financial institutions were required to calculate caps for their wire transfer operations. The use of this method of transferring money is likely to continue to increase. It is the most efficient way of moving money from one area to another.

Now, checkbook money has almost disappeared from large and urgent transactions. Where banks formerly wrote drafts (a form of check), now they instruct a clerk to enter the transaction on the computer terminal. There is no float and the transaction is final and handled in minutes, with no kiting, either. But as with any transaction there is the opportunity for fraud: clerks handling these transfers are carefully screened for honesty and integrity, security around the equipment and the related facilities is monitored carefully, and access to the equipment is by code and the code is changed frequently.

Where did our checkbook money go? It is still here. In 1986, check volume was continuing to increase at the rate of 4 to 6 percent annually. Printers of checkbooks were reporting a record volume of orders. The fast checkout line at the supermarket says "cash only," but the other lines accept checks and many customers use them. A few stores are attempting to install "point of sale" equipment. With this, the customer presents an identification card which the clerk inserts into a computer terminal. This quickly charges the customer's account at the financial institution and credits the store's account. No float, no kiting, no paper to get lost, and no checkbook to carry.

But customers are not eager to use this procedure, preferring to give a check that will not reach their bank for at least a day. And if a weekend or holiday is involved it could be several days, time enough to make a deposit, if necessary, to cover the check. Besides, keeping a record of money spent is easy with the checkbook. A name for the check written and cashed Friday evening when no funds are in the account, but will be Monday, is "weekend debentures."

Checkbook money has not gone away; it is still very much a part of our money system and from every indication at this point in time it will be around a long time. However, its use between businesses and banks is declining rapidly. The use of computers to handle payrolls, government checks, and other regular payments improves efficiency, reduces losses, and makes record keeping easier and cheaper. The use of automated clearinghouse arrangements where transfers of money are processed on magnetic tapes by computers skyrocketed during the 1970s and 1980s. It eliminates paper and greatly reduces cost of transportation; the image on a magnetic tape can be sent over the wire. It can be prepared ahead of time and rarely gets lost. Direct deposit of government and payroll checks to the payee's account is rapidly taking the place of checks. Still, not everyone wants his deposit to go directly to his bank. Some people just like to "feel" that check in their hand. As one banker put it, "what else do they have to do but to go to the post office, pick up their check, go to the bank, wait in line for thirty minutes and deposit their check?" During this time they have visited with friends, caught up with the latest gossip and had an enjoyable morning.

Chapter Five
Credit Cards

Their Origins

"I didn't bring our checkbook and I don't have enough cash with me to buy that suit," might be a comment of a husband to his wife as they find a sharp-looking suit on sale.

"You have our VISA card, don't you? I noticed on the front door that they accept VISA and Mastercharge cards," replied his wife.

What would we do without our charge cards? They enable us to make purchases for goods on sale and to defer the charge to our supply of money for several days — maybe even weeks, and in some cases with no service or interest charge. The growth in the use of credit cards has been nothing less than phenomenal. In 1983 there were nearly 600 million credit card accounts and seven out of ten households possessed at least one. Outstanding balances in these accounts totaled more than $75 billion, an amount equal to nearly 3 percent of the gross national product. The dollar volume of transactions via credit cards was much higher, probably exceeding twice the outstanding amount. This dollar volume equals or exceeds the $148 billion of currency in circulation and probably represents a third of all retail sales.

Credit cards have been around for a long time, but only since 1950 have they become a common means of paying for goods. Prior to this date, individual stores, oil companies and hotels often issued their own credit card to customers with well-established credit, but use was limited to a small portion of the population. The use of these special cards grew until halted by the Great Depression of the 1930s, and because of credit restrictions, they were rarely used during World War II.

In the late 1940s and early 1950s their use again became popular but still each company or store issued its own card and it was good only at its store. If you wanted to use a credit card at a JC Penney's, you had to have a Penney's credit card. Stores and hotels with many locations accepted credit cards issued by their parent company but not those of others. In addition to credit cards, most of these companies offered charge accounts to selected customers.

In 1938 the major oil companies agreed to honor each other's credit cards, thus making it possible to travel across the country by auto and carry a minimum amount of cash. This was the first national credit card arrangement.

In 1950, Frank McNamara, then head of Hamilton Credit Corporation, a small commercial finance company in New York, decided that credit cards would be more useful if they were accepted by many different places of business. He was especially interested in having a card that would be widely accepted by restaurants, hotels and nightclubs. His original Diners Club card was accepted at twenty-eight of Manhattan's top restaurants and nightclubs. This first general-purpose card was made of cardboard with the member's name and account number on one side and the list of participating restaurants on the back.

This venture was so successful that Mr. McNamara's attorney, Ralph Schneider, and his publicist, Matty Simmons, arranged a merger with Dine and Sign, a West Coast dining and entertaining plan financed by department store heir Alfred Bloomingdale. A few years later, Mr. Schneider and Mr. Bloomingdale bought the company from Mr. McNamara for $500,000. In the meantime, Diners Club was accepted at about 2,000 establishments. In 1955, the cardboard card was replaced by plastic. Expanding again in the mid–1960s, Diners joined up with Fugazy Travel. Then followed the election of George Faunce, III, as chairman and in 1970 Diners was purchased by Continental Corporation. In June 1981 Citicorp bought Diners Club from Continental and it became a part of Citicorp Service Division of the Consumer Banking Travel and Entertainment Group of Citibank. With the success of Diners Club card others soon followed. American Express and Carte Blanche were probably the best known.

Plastic money was still limited by the fact that many stores did not accept it. Except for auto supplies at service stations and purchases at stores which had issued their own cards, most purchases were with cash or, if credit had been established on account, payable in thirty days. Also, many of the credit cards such as Diners Club and American Express made a monthly charge for the privilege of using the card. Sometimes this was an annual charge and sometimes it was a one-time charge for issuing the card.

Bank Cards

Enter commercial banks. Seeing much of its consumer credit business going to others such as stores, oil companies and travel companies, in 1951 the Franklin National Bank in New York issued its own credit card. During the period of 1951 to 1958, the idea grew, with twenty-six banks offering them in 1957. Together they had 754,000 card holders and 11,000 participating merchants. Dollar volume was $40 million and the average annual dollar volume per customer was $53.

In the beginning banks relied on a percentage discount from merchants to cover the cost of the credit card operation. This discount started at about 6 percent but competition soon brought it down to less than 3 percent. At this level, it did not cover the cost of operating the card program. As a result, it became apparent to banks that the only way the operation could be profitable was for most of their card holders to utilize the "revolving" credit plan and pay only a minimum amount each month. The outstanding balance would be earning interest at the profitable consumer credit rate — usually 18 percent annually. The bank's first attempt at marketing the cards was to send out thousands of unsolicited cards to persons who were expected to have a good credit rating. This biased the mailing to middle and higher income families who would pay the entire bill within the thirty day "free" no-interest period. The next step was to try to reach the lower-income families who still had sufficient income to be a good credit risk but would take advantage of the revolving account and thus pay a substantial interest charge.

In addition, in order for the program to be profitable it was necessary to have a high volume of transactions. This meant sending out thousands of unsolicited cards and then screening the users as their payment habits became known. This attempt to gain a large number of cardholders led to indiscriminate mailings and consumers complained about all the credit cards they received. There was fear that someone else would gain possession of them and make charges that the intended holder would have to pay. In the late 1970s Congress passed legislation requiring that the card issuer receive a request from the prospective holder before issuing a card, and limiting liability of the card holder to $50 if he gave prompt notice of the loss of a card.

In the 1950s several banks on the East Coast started a credit card program; on the West Coast one bank — Bank of America — initiated such a program. The fact that branch banking was permitted on the West Coast, particularly in California, was a major factor in the fact that Bank of America's program boomed while those banks on the East Coast, for the most part, gave up the idea. Chase Manhattan Bank, one of the largest, after four years sold its credit card business. Without numerous branches over which the parent bank had control, it was not possible to generate the necessary volume for a profitable operation. In California the name Bank of America was synonymous with banking throughout the state. Thus, a customer in San Diego could use his BankAmericard in San Francisco or any other part of the state. Lack of branch banking in the East made such widespread acceptance impossible.

Even with the advantage of branch banking, Bank of America did not even keep separate records of its credit card operation until 1961. At that time, it had one million card holders, 35,000 merchants participating and an annual volume of business of $75 million. Six years later there were 2.7 million card holders, 83,000 merchants and an annual volume of $335 million.

The success Bank of America had with credit cards was fine for them but small independent banks could not make their programs profitable because of the low volume. Answer? Join the Bank of America program. Thus, in 1966 Bank of America offered to franchise its card through a separate corporation known as BankAmericard Service Corporation. By January 1970, a total of 3,301 banks throughout the United States and in foreign countries had affiliated themselves with the BankAmericard scheme.

Affiliating with BankAmericard had its drawbacks; Bank of America held tight control over the program. For example, the local bank could not decide which of its customers would receive the card. This restriction by Bank of America led to the organization of a regional association of banks to provide their own credit card. It would still give wider acceptance than if offered by individual banks and yet give more control to the local bank. In a short time these associations organized into one group that became issuers of a single card called Master Card.

The bank credit card opened up a wide field of participation. As the acceptance of credit cards grew, more and more merchants found it to their advantage to accept cards. Also, customers found themselves with a pocketful of plastic cards. Billfolds and purses bulged not with money but with credit cards. Soon consumers asked themselves—and some merchants—why do I have to carry so many cards? Why can't everyone accept at least one of the national and internationally known credit cards?

By the mid-1980s, this question was being answered by the two major bank cards with VISA (the sequel to BankAmericard) and Master Charge being widely accepted by merchants. And American Express, Carte Blanche and Diners moved into the retail area. Thus, a customer with Visa, Mastercharge or American Express Card could almost travel the world without any cash.

Use and Attitude Toward Credit Cards

The use of credit cards has been the subject of several studies. One completed in 1971 by Lewis Mandel gives information on "Who uses credit cards?" Personal interviews were conducted with 3,880 heads of families throughout the United States. One of the first things found was that about half of all families used at least one credit card. Income was a major determinant as to the use of a credit card, and it may seem surprising that the higher income families were more likely to use the cards than were those with a lower income. For example, when family income was $25,000 or more, 80 percent of the families used a credit card. In families with less than $3,000 annual income only 17 percent used a credit card. Not too surprising, families with even lower income did not use cards as they might not have been able to qualify for one. It should be remembered that this was in 1971 and the use of credit cards has changed substantially since then.

One reason for the greater use by higher income families is that a larger proportion of their spending is for goods and not for food. At this time, most grocery stores are not accepting credit cards. Another fact revealed by this study is that younger families (in reference to age) were more frequent users of credit cards. These were the families with the greatest need and thus more likely to need extra credit. This was especially true of young families with children.

Geographic location also was an important factor in the use of credit cards. Suburban families near large cities were the largest group of users with three-fourths of families in this category using cards. Next came the suburbs of smaller cities and at the bottom of the list were rural and small-town residents. West Coast residents were more likely to use the cards than other areas of the United States. The program of Bank of America probably accounted for the heavy use on the West Coast. Again it should be noted that these data are for 1970 and 1971. As the use of cards became more widespread, many of these differences no doubt disappeared. By the mid–1980s, as noted earlier, more than 70 percent of all families used credit cards. As usage became more widespread, credit card money became almost universal.

The study by Mandel included questions regarding attitudes toward the use of credit cards. Questions such as "Is it a good idea to use credit cards?" brought out the fact that nearly one-third of the families interviewed felt that it was bad business to use credit cards. The response varied depending on the type of card, with bank cards receiving the most negative votes. Even of those who used credit cards, nearly one-fifth said it was "bad."

A study in 1983 by the Federal Reserve Board did not include this aspect of the use of cards, but the much higher usage suggests that these attitudes may have changed. The usual reason for giving credit cards a negative vote was that they encourage spending beyond the capacity of the cardholder to pay. They provided very easy credit and it required a high degree of self-discipline to avoid overspending. Young people say that they have had to cut up their credit cards to avoid overspending.

Users of credit cards were divided into two categories by the 1983 study: convenience users and installment users. The first group used their cards because it permitted them to carry less cash and also to defer payment, sometimes by as much as forty-five days. This permitted the holder to make purchases when items were on sale whether or not the holder had adequate cash at the moment. Also, when traveling it was a big advantage not only to reduce the amount of cash needed but to obtain instant credit anywhere the cards were accepted.

"Installment users" found that credit cards enabled them to extend their credit and to spread out repayments. Using the revolving plan where a minimum payment is due each month, they could "bridge" over from one period to another. If income was low in one month, payment of the total due could be deferred and only the minimum amount paid. Later, as funds became available, the balance could be paid. This is certainly not a firm division, as each person in each category may at times use his cards for the other reason.

One of the questions addressed by the 1983 study was whether the use of credit cards actually increased total spending. Some people had assumed that because credit cards provided readily available credit, the total spending of a family would be higher than without the cards. The study found that there was no significant evidence that total spending did increase. Usually, an impulse purchase was offset by denying a later purchase. This suggests that most use of credit cards is for convenience and not for extending credit or increasing expenditures.

Following is a quote from the 1983 survey that reflects attitudes and reasons for use of credit cards:

> To obtain some notion of the possible link between credit cards, unplanned or impulsive purchases, and changes in a household's total spending, the Federal Reserve commissioned the Survey Research Center to include several special questions on this subject in its January 1983 monthly survey of households. The answers to these questions did not indicate an especially strong connection between credit card usage and household spending, a result consistent with the finding from other surveys that about one-half of card-holding households typically use cards for convenience rather than to augment purchasing power on a longer-term basis through installment use.
>
> In the January 1983 survey, respondents were first asked if in the past three months they had made any purchase larger than $20 that they "had not planned to shop for when [they] went into the store." Respondents were then asked for each instance mentioned what they had purchased, the price of the item, why they had made the purchase, and whether they had done so with cash, check or credit card. Those who had used a credit card were then asked if they would have purchased the item had they not had a credit card, and if not, whether they would have purchased the item within the next few months.
>
> Forty-one percent of the survey respondents indicated that they had made at least one unplanned purchase of $20 or larger in the preceding three months. About 40 percent of those respondents reported more than one planned purchase. The most common unplanned purchase fell in the broad category of clothing, jewelry, and personal items, followed by household items including major durables. Hobby, recreational, and educational items comprised the next largest category. The purchased items covered a broad price range. Twenty-five and thirty dollars were the most frequently mentioned amounts (for the first purchase discussed), but 35 percent mentioned purchase amounts of $100 or more, and almost 7 percent reported purchases of $500 or more.
>
> For each unplanned purchase, respondents were asked "What was the main reason that you decided to purchase the item at that time?" Not surprisingly nearly half the respondents answered that they "needed/wanted/liked" the item purchased. After all, any purchase presumably is made in order to meet some perceived need or desire, even if the perception of that need develops only a few moments in advance of the purchase. Some of the other responses were also need-related — for example, some said the item was purchased to replace an

older item that was "worn out" or "needed replacing anyway." The primary reason for purchase not directly related to need was attractive pricing of the item, variously described as being "on sale," a "bargain," or a "good deal." Thirty percent of the respondents cited this reason. Thirteen percent said they bought the item as a gift or "to surprise someone." Reasons mentioned by less than 2 percent of the respondents were that they "had extra money" or that the item "was hard to find" elsewhere or at other times.

A particularly interesting result of the survey is that only slightly more than one-fourth of those making an unplanned purchase used a credit card to do so. Unfortunately, no "control group" data exist on the proportion of planned purchases made by credit card in the relevant categories (clothing and personal, household goods, hobby and recreational). Still, a frequency of one card purchase in four would not seem to establish a particularly strong relationship between unplanned purchases and credit card use. A full 70 percent of the unplanned purchases were made either by cash (52 percent) or by check (18 percent). About 3 percent were made by other, unidentified, means. When purchases were classified by size, the incidence of card use appeared to increase as purchases became larger, but not to a striking extent. For unplanned purchases above $100, 31 percent were transacted by credit card compared with 25 percent for transactions of $100 or less.

In all (considering only the first item mentioned), 70 respondents made an unplanned purchase by credit card. Forty of these purchasers (57 percent) said they would have made the purchase at the time even if they had not carried a credit card — they were not asked how — and 30 respondents (43 percent) said they would not have made the purchase at that time without their credit card. Finally, the 30 respondents who would not have made the purchase were asked if they would have made it within the next few months — 19 said yes, they would have, and 11 said no.

Responses to hypothetical questions, of course, have considerable limitations. Statements as to what one would do if circumstances were different entail varying degrees of reliability for different respondents. Still, in the absence of a compelling reason to suspect a large bias in the answers provided, the survey results suggest that in only a small number of cases might credit cards ultimately prove decisive in the completion of an unplanned purchase. Seventy-three percent of the unplanned purchases studied were transacted by means other than credit card; another 15 percent would have been made at the same time even without access to a card, and another 7 percent would have been carried out at some later time. Only 4 percent of all the completed purchases (11 of 259), or 16 percent of credit card purchases (11 of 70), would never have been made without a credit card, in the judgment of the purchasers themselves.

Unplanned purchases, of course, represent only a fraction of total purchases. If the above proportions are reasonably accurate, it seems likely that far less than 4 percent of all purchases — planned and unplanned — could be described as sales that would never have taken place at all without credit cards. Moreover, even for those unanticipated purchases identified as entirely dependent on credit cards, it is still not possible to say that they represent a net addition to total spending. In the absence of the card-dependent purchases and subsequent payment to them, it may be that different purchases would have been made at some point, so that the total spending and total saving of the individuals would have been the same over time in either case.

Remember our old friend the checkbook? By the mid–1980s, some banks were offering their credit card holders the privilege of writing checks against their credit cards! Just write a check and we will charge, not your checking account, but your credit card account. Why this reversion to that centuries-old method of using money? Very simple: the company offering the privilege of writing checks against a credit card account is also one of those that does not have a free thirty-day period to pay your bill. Interest begins to accrue the day the charge is entered on the credit card account. So here they are offering the customer a little float for the privilege of the card issuer earning some more interest.

Chapter Six
Credit

Early Use

A man who had lived in the same town for several years complained that he could not get a credit card or borrow from the bank even though he had always paid his bills promptly. He rented an apartment where the landlord paid the utility bills so he had no record with the utility company. Upon questioning, it developed that he had always paid cash for everything. He did not have a checking account nor had he ever borrowed money. He had never used "invisible" money, and lenders were reluctant to extend credit to him because he had no record of promptly repaying a loan. Paying cash for each purchase left no *written* record of his great habit of paying bills promptly.

Contrast this with another friend who, upon reaching the age where he was earning some of his own money, went to his bank and made a small loan, partly on the reputation of his family. He did not really need the money so he put the proceeds of the loan in a savings account and when the loan became due, he withdrew the savings and paid the loan. He made it a point to borrow small sums from time to time and always repaid them promptly. In this way he established a written record of his credit. He had used invisible money and had references to show that he was a good credit risk.

A banker with many years of experience in lending money said that the first question he asked of a prospective customer who wanted to borrow money is "Where have you borrowed before?" If the answer is at least one place, he could quickly check the borrower's record of repayment. Without it he has to rely on his gut feeling about the borrower's reputation for repaying a loan.

The extension of credit — the creation of invisible money — probably is as old as man himself. Ancient man probably loaned his favorite club to a neighbor or he may have given him a share of his meat in return for a promise to share a future kill by his friend. Certainly the early Chinese, Greeks and Romans made ample use of credit. The citizens of ancient Babylon were noted for being shrewd merchants and credit would have been an integral part of their operations. As we saw in earlier chapters, merchants and bankers in

England in the sixteenth century extended credit as a part of their efforts to meet the needs of the people.

Early use of bills of exchange by merchants and the willingness to defer payment for goods for a period of time — ten days or thirty days, for example, was a form of invisible money. In the sixteenth, seventeenth and eighteenth centuries, and to some extent today, the widespread use of bills associated with trade transactions enabled economies to operate with less coin or currency. As a sale of goods was made to a merchant and he gave in return his confirmation of the transaction, usually a "bill," he initiated a piece of paper that could be endorsed by the seller to a third party and then to another and another until the same piece of paper had served to facilitate many transactions with no money involved. When the first purchaser sold the goods, he would pay the original seller or whoever held the bill at that time. When the bankers entered the picture it often made the operation much easier, as they had many contacts with merchants and the original seller could readily discount, or sell, his bill to the bank. The bank in turn could use funds placed on deposit to pay the seller. The question of whether credit is money occupied many discussions among eighteenth-century writers and tradesmen. Charles List in his *History of Monetary and Credit Theory* cites comments by Adam Smith, Ricardo, Mollien and Tooks. He gives considerable space to the theories of John Law and his activities with the Bank of France, and his idea that money created wealth. Most of the theories of today on money and credit were discussed by the writers of the eighteenth and nineteenth centuries. At first, bank notes — currency issued by banks — were not considered credit, but in time they were accepted as a type of credit. When a bank issued its notes it was in effect extending credit against the metallic coin which it held. As depositors placed their coins with the bank and the bank issued a receipt (counterpart of today's certificate of deposit), the depositors were actually loaning funds to the bank.

Invisible money, credit, literally runs the business world today. Consider the fact that at the end of June 1985, loans at commercial banks alone totaled one and a half trillion dollars. Investments, primarily in bonds, were over two trillion dollars. Add to this $260 billion in commercial paper, $500 billion in consumer credit and billions in accounts receivable and accounts payable, and the importance of invisible money becomes apparent. Even if the $180 billion in currency was used many times over it still would not come close to meeting the needs of the business world.

Allocation of Credit

Allocation of credit has become an accepted role of government in many areas. In the United States, government agencies created by Congress extend credit to farmers, ranchers, businesses, and consumers. The report of the United States Treasury for the first quarter of 1984 shows outstanding credit by these agencies at $7 billion. The bulk of this amount was to assist family housing through the Federal Housing Administration. Other agencies, although not directly tied to the federal government, include Farm Credit banks, Federal Home Loan banks, Federal Land banks and Banks for Cooperatives. These agencies borrow money from the public by issuing securities and then loan the funds to farmers and others. Amounts of these loans in 1984 totaled more than $140 billion.

This indirect allocation of credit began in the 1920s and was given a big push in the legislation of the 1930s during the Great Depression. These agencies effectively direct a substantial portion of credit each year.

A more severe regulation of credit is found in Mexico. In that nation, the central bank, Banco de Mexico, monitors the loans of commercial banks and tells the banks what proportion of their loans can be for certain purposes. Failure to comply brings strict retribution from the central bank. In the United States direct allocation of credit through commercial banks has taken a more subtle approach. Bank examiners evaluate the distribution of a bank's loans and usually will criticize those that are out of the bank's trade area, or that are for highly speculative purposes. A more direct guide is found in the Community Reinvestment Act of 1977; this act directs banks to include loans to all segments of the community. The ratio is determined by the mix of the population in the bank's trade area. Failure to comply can result in loss of all government accounts including the account for withheld taxes—a large account in many banks.

Credit Regulations

The importance of invisible money to the nation and its economic progress is illustrated by the attempts that have been made to control it through government regulation. Invisible money encourages spending and since it is used for purchasing a wide range of products, regulating it can help direct spending in a specific direction.

During World War II, strict regulations were invoked in the United States to direct spending in a path desired by the government as it sought to direct every effort to the successful execution of the war. Generally, these regulations sought to reduce spending for consumer goods that were in short supply. Also, reducing spending for consumer goods tended to encourage purchase of War Bonds.

Two regulations were used to administer these controls. Regulation W related to consumer credit, and it specified the amount of down payment, length of pay-out and methods of determining prices for most consumer goods. For example, a consumer buying a used car could not obtain financing for more than two-thirds of the "bona fide" purchase price. The regulation then took nearly a column of fine print to define bona fide purchase price. Virtually every consumer good was included under the regulation, and criminal penalties could be assessed if the violation of the regulation was intentional. Federal Reserve banks were given the task of administering the regulations and representatives from the banks inspected records of thousands of firms selling used cars, refrigerators, radios, stoves, and hundreds of other consumer goods.

Regulation X covered transactions involving repairs and remodeling of homes. Again, down payments and pay-out periods were specified for any material repair or remodeling of a residence. This regulation came late in the war effort and was a further attempt to control invisible money and channel every available resource into winning the war.

These regulations were activated again in 1950 during the Korean conflict. Enforcement had been difficult during World War II but the problem of enforcement during the Korean conflict was almost insurmountable.

There was a strong patriotic feeling during World War II as the war dragged on and people felt an obligation to voluntarily comply with the regulations. The so-called police action in Korea stirred very little patriotism and in fact, memory of shortages during World War II spurred many to rush out and buy new refrigerators, stoves, and other consumer goods ahead of the regulations. Federal Reserve banks were again given the job of administering the regulation and inspecting for compliance. The regulations were lifted soon as the Korean War dragged on and the involvement of the United States did not make as large a drain on the nation's resources as had been anticipated.

The difficulty of controlling invisible money is illustrated by the hundreds of interpretations required for the regulations and the ingenuity of the public to find loopholes. Following the first amendment to Regulation W in October 1941, there were listed in the Federal Reserve Bulletin of the Board of Governors interpretations numbered 16 through 93. This was only the beginning. Every day for weeks additional interpretations had to be made: "Was a station wagon the same as a car and would it be covered by the regulation?" "Yes. It is covered." "Are used cars covered?" "Yes." On and on the questions came as John Q. Public sought ways of circumventing the regulation or honest persons wanted to be sure they were in compliance.

From time to time Congress has passed legislation providing for allocation of credit. In December 1969 it passed an act that gave the president standby powers to authorize the Federal Reserve System to "regulate and control any and all extensions of credit" when he (the president) deems such action to be appropriate for controlling inflation. This act was used briefly in May 1980. The Federal Reserve published guidelines for the allocation of credit and limiting its use. Credit cards were included and total bank loans were severely limited. The impact was immediate and so drastic as to plunge the economy into a temporary recession. By the middle of June it was apparent that the controls were no longer needed and they were gradually lifted.

In 1976 Congress passed the Humphrey-Hawkins Bill, entitled the Full

Employment and Balanced Growth Act of 1976, which called for the following: "A monetary policy designed to assure such rate of growth in the Nation's
money supply, such interest rates, and such availability, including policies of
credit reform, allocation and international capital flows as are conducive to the
achieving and maintaining the full employment production, purchasing
power and priority goals specified earlier [in the bill]."

In addition, the Credit and Uses Reporting Act of 1975 implicitly gave
priority status to "productive capital investment, farms, and small business
firms, housing and other purposes, including the accommodation of consumer
credit needs basic to a rising standard of living for American families." As if this
wasn't enough, Senator Sweiker's (R, Penn.) bill, S.887, added the following:
"The provision of capital for investment in plant and equipment where necessary
to assure adequate supplies of essential commodities; the provision of capital for
investment necessary to create new jobs, prevent unemployment, or inflationary
prices; and such additional purposes as the Board [of Governors of the Federal
Reserve System] determines to be appropriate in order to assure stable and
balanced economic growth by the most efficient use of available credit."

As of this writing there are no direct credit controls in effect and the broad
authority given to the president to institute such controls has expired. But
these illustrations indicate the vital importance of this invisible money in the
business world today. And the importance that government gives to its use.
The allocation of this form of money is sure to be used again and again in an
attempt to direct resources into specific areas to achieve political and/or socio-
logical goals.

Advantages of Credit

Some of the advantages of invisible money to individuals are obvious. A
young married couple could not possibly save enough money quickly to pay
for a house; it could take a lifetime to do so. But with the use of credit — a
mortgage — they can have the privilege of living in a house that they call their
own with a very small down payment of cash. Most purchasers of new cars could
not pay cash for that necessity in today's world; credit enables them to buy now
and pay as it is used. Almost every business begins by borrowing part of the
capital needed to begin operations. In the early years of our industrial economy
it was possible to begin a business with very little capital, but that is not so today. One of our favorite examples is in agriculture. For many years the requirements for starting a farming operation were a mule, a plow and plenty of hard
work, and an investment of a few hundred dollars; in many cases these could
be borrowed from a friend or relative. The land could be leased or rented for
a share of the crops. In time, the beginning farmer could save enough to make
a down payment on some land and if fortune smiled on him, he could, in a
lifetime, own his own farm and equipment.

Not so today. To compete in modern agriculture requires more than a subsistence operation. Machinery has taken the place of the mule. The equipment needed now includes plows, cultivating and harvesting equipment, and frequently, storage facilities. The smallest tractor may cost several thousand dollars. It is conservatively estimated that a minimum of $100,000 is needed just for basic equipment. Land can still be rented for a share of the crops but a profitable operation requires several hundred acres as opposed to forty with the mule. And land prices have skyrocketed beyond a level that is justified for reasonable profits from farming or ranching.

Dr. Karl Wright, professor emeritus at Michigan State University, writing in the 1984 publication *Futures* states that "If you're going to make it farming, you have to be small and have an off-farm job, or big enough (over 500 acres) to be able to operate efficiently." We could cite other examples of business and industry. The dollar amounts would be even greater.

Invisible money plays a vital role in another phase of our modern economy. Commodity and stock markets have been criticized for being only a gambling operation. But these markets serve a useful purpose in providing a ready market for the movement of goods, for establishing a market value for commodities and for the common stock of corporations. In addition, they provide a means of hedging regular operations that require the use of raw materials such as grain, oil and fibers. These markets could not function without the ample use of invisible money. For example, in commodities, a 10 percent payment is all that is required in some purchases. Thus, with $1,000 you can control $10,000 in the market. This gives tremendous leverage and permits many persons to participate and helps broaden the market. Investments in the stock market often can be financed with only a 50 percent down payment.

The importance of invisible money is also reflected in the huge amounts of debt owed by citizens and governments of the United States. At the end of 1983 total debt of individuals and governments as reported by the Federal Reserve System was $5,656.1 billion dollars—60 percent more than the total gross national product. Of this total, 40 percent was owed by individuals, about 20 percent represented debt of the Federal government, and state and local governments held another 7 percent. These relationships have not changed materially since 1970. They have fluctuated from year to year but even since the period from 1950 the percentages show a fairly consistent trend.

Consumers have come into the debt picture mostly since the 1930s. In 1919 consumer debt, except mortgages, was only 2 percent of the total private debt. The proportion increased steadily until 1960 when it reached the level of about 10 percent, a level that has prevailed into the mid–1980s. Prior to 1920, borrowing by individuals was usually for mortgage money or for operating a business. For many years individuals were about the only source of invisible money for consumers. Following World War II and particularly after the Monetary Control Act of 1980, lending has become a part of the operation of hundreds of businesses. Insurance companies have always been active in the mortgage market but by the mid–1980s they were involved in development loans, loans to policy holders and a multitude of joint ventures. Also, as a result of the Monetary Control Act of 1980, virtually all lenders—banks, savings and loan associations, credit unions, bankers, insurance companies and even major corporations such as Sears have broadened their operations in the consumer lending area.

How to Obtain Credit

Volumes have been written on the use of credit, how to obtain it and how to control it. For the purposes of this discussion we can say it is another form of money and one that is essential to modern business. It is an integral part of our society. Obtaining it is relatively easy if you follow a few simple rules.

Remember that the major concern—in fact, about the only concern except for the desire for some income from the loan—of a lender is that the loan be repaid. No one likes to lose money and if the prospective lender has doubts about the borrower's ability or willingness to repay, the loan is not likely to be made. How does a lender evaluate the chances of a loan being repaid? What questions should the prospective borrower of this invisible money be prepared to answer?

Bankers often quote the three "C's" of credit evaluation—character, collateral and capacity. And many will insist that the first "C" is the only one of importance. Collateral is, just for the record, in case you get hit by a truck or suddenly decide to skip the country. Capacity to repay a loan is added insurance.

By character, lenders mean the desire and intention to repay the invisible money. Collateral is what they might sell to collect the invisible money if necessary. Capacity is your ability to repay the loan from resources, including your ability to use the money profitably. Most lenders want to know how you plan to use the funds; they want to feel that its use will provide a reasonable chance of enabling you to repay. If the borrower has a well-established reputation for repaying debts and has a strong financial statement that gives assurance that regardless of the use of the money he can repay from other assets, the lender may not be too concerned with the use to be made of the invisible money. A signature loan, which uses no collateral, is more likely to come from a relative who wants to help a relative get started in a business. Even most loans made on signature only are backed by a strong financial statement if the loan is from a financial institution.

So if you want to make maximum use of invisible money, be prepared to assure the provider of that money that you are honest, that you intend to repay the money, that you have a sound reason for needing the money and that you are willing to pay the going rate of interest for the use of this invisible money.

Suppose you have all the requirements for being an acceptable borrower and the lender still says "no." Sometimes the money is not available. Financial institutions sometimes are "loaned up"—all their funds are already invested. Sometimes the use you plan to make of the funds is illegal or contrary to regulations. For example, under certain conditions financial institutions are required by law not to loan more than a certain percent of the purchase price of certain securities. This percentage varies from time to time but it does restrict the amount that can be loaned for this purpose. Other regulations restrict the decisions officers of these institutions can make in loaning money.

Invisible money is the partner of many a successful business. It opens doors, bridges over financial crises and extends the horizons of a business or an individual. It creates new opportunities and a hundred other features make it essential to the operation of today's business and to the consumer. Such a "friend" should be treated with "love and affection." Carefully and honestly developed and nurtured it serves its master well. Mistreated, it becomes a chain and ball that will eventually be the downfall of the most talented manager. Above all, treat it honestly, and do not overuse it. Most of the time an individual or a business should be able to pay off any debt by liquidating assets if that becomes necessary. Each type of business has guidelines that have proven effective through experience. For example, airlines traditionally have a large ratio of debt to assets, but most retail operations need a smaller ratio of debt to assets. The rule of two to one—twice as many liquid assets as short term debt—applies to many operations. More about individual use of credit in Chapter Nine.

Chapter Seven
Creation and Control of Money

Money Creation and Supply

Create money? Sounds like fun, doesn't it? It actually happens in the operation of a financial institution that accepts demand deposits and makes loans. We are not talking about currency and coin, of course. We have already seen how those are printed or struck, and that the amount printed or struck depends on the cash demands of the business community and consumers.

Creating money in the operation of a financial institution—a bank, savings and loan association or credit union—happens because most borrowers do not demand cash at the time they negotiate a loan. The more common practice is to have the bank credit the borrower's checking account, and then the borrower writes checks against the account as the need arises. This may be over a period of a few days or months or even years in some cases. Usually, the money will be used within a matter of days or weeks. For example, a contractor borrows $100,000, signs a note for that amount and the lender credits the borrower's checking account for $100,000. That afternoon the contractor pays a bill for $1,000 for materials by mailing a check to a supplier. It may take a few days for the check to reach the borrower's bank and in the meantime, the amount of deposits at the borrower's bank has been increased by $100,000. When the $1,000 check arrives at the bank and is paid, deposits are reduced by that amount.

Anytime a financial institution that accepts demand deposits buys a security or makes a loan, deposits are increased either at the lending institution or at another similar institution. Somewhere in the chain of business transactions demand deposits are increased. To illustrate again, when a bank buys a United States government bond, it pays the government for the bond. The government deposits the money in a Federal Reserve Bank and writes checks against the deposit. As the government checks are cashed by payees at least some part of it will be in the form of a demand deposit. It is very rare that all of the checks written would be cashed for cash; almost always a part of the funds will be deposited in a checking account.

If financial institutions can create money so easily, what prevents them from creating an unlimited supply of it? Several factors limit their operations. For one, they are regulated and must place a portion of each deposit in a reserve account. This may be with the Federal Reserve Bank or other supervisory agency. Also, they can only make loans if someone wants to borrow, and loans will not be made if the prospective borrower is not a good credit risk. One of the great deterrents to reckless operations is the fact that any demand deposit must be made available to the depositor when he asks for it. Demand deposits mean just that — on demand. So the institution must be prepared at all times to honor any request for demand funds. In commercial banks, an amount equal to about 5 percent of total deposits is needed in cash to meet demands of customers. Although demand deposits are not coin or currency, they are a major part of the money supply of the nation, and in that sense, are real money.

This is an appropriate time to talk about the money supply. It is a term used by economists and others to describe the potential spending power available to the public at any given time. This will include coins, currency, checking accounts, savings accounts, money market funds, certificates of deposit and any other immediately available funds. Because some funds, like cash in your pocket, can be spent easier than others, such as a certificate of deposit, economists have devised different classes of money. As of this writing, there are four classifications. These definitions have varied from time to time and may again in the future.

> **M-1** the sum of currency (and coin) in circulation, demand deposits, traveler's checks and other checkable deposits.
> **M-2** M-1 *plus* money market fund balances, savings and small time deposits, overnight repurchase agreements and Eurodollars and money market mutual funds.
> **M-3** All of the above *plus* large time deposits, term repurchase agreements, term Eurodollars and institutions money market mutual funds.
> **L** All of the above *plus* other liquid assets.

Control of Money

Now let's move on to the control of money; we could call this discussion "printing press" money. But control of money is a much broader subject and deserves consideration of many aspects of the subject. It will, however, include references to printing press money.

One of the problems in controlling money is the fact that if two forms of money equal in debt-paying value but unequal in intrinsic value are circulating at the same time, the less valuable tends to remain in circulation and the other hoarded or exported as bullion. This is known as Gresham's law. Stated another way, bad money drives out good money. Sir Thomas Gresham

(1519–1579) was an English merchant and founder of the Royal Exchange in London. He attended Caius College in Cambridge and later became a very successful merchant. Living in Antwerp for a time, he represented the British government in negotiating new loans, the repayment of matured loans and occasionally the shipment of specie to England. He was consistently successful in public and private ventures even if his methods were sometimes high-handed and questionable.

The principle expressed in Gresham's law had been well known by 1550 and had been stated by several, including Nicolaus Copernicus (1473–1543) in his essay on coinage. In England an obscure author, Humphrey Holt, in 1551 bewailed the fact that the heavier coins were being hoarded or exported, leaving only the lesser coins in circulation. However, by virtue of Gresham's title and his prominence in financial matters, he is given credit for discovering the principle and textbooks from that day have unapologetically credited him with this "great" statement.

According to the *Encyclopaedia Britannica,* Gresham's major contribution was his proposal to Queen Elizabeth in 1558 to establish an equalization fund to support the exchange rate of the English pound. Since the Queen did not have the necessary 10,000 pounds to create such a fund, she rejected it.

Some examples of Gresham's law have operated in the United States. About 1777, the Continental paper money (with no backing in specie) began to depreciate rapidly. People hoarded their gold, silver, and copper coins and endeavored to spend the depreciated currency. During President Van Buren's administration (March 4, 1837–March 3, 1841), and during the Civil War, people took almost all of the United States coin out of circulation. They hoarded the coins because they were afraid the paper money had no value. The Coinage Act of 1965 eliminated silver from U.S. dimes and quarters, and reduced the silver content of the half-dollars to 40 percent. Soon thereafter, silver coins (those dated prior to 1965) began to rapidly disappear from sight.

Control of money is one of the functions of government. Dictators and emperors have found this to be one of the most useful tools of their realm, and democracies and republics make it a central part of their government structures. A government-created bank is usually the device used to exert this control.

The Bank of Norway was the first established central bank, opening in 1668, but private banking did not begin in Norway until 1830. The first "recognized" central bank was the Bank of England, established in 1694. Sometimes referred to as the "Little Old Lady of Threadneedle Street" because of its conservative policies and its location on Threadneedle Street in London, the bank has served as a pattern for central banks throughout the world.

Other central banks and dates of establishment include the Bank of Ireland, 1783; Bank of Montreal (Canada), 1822; Bank of France, 1800; National Bank of Belgium, 1850; Bank of Prussia, 1846 (later renamed the Reichsbank in 1875 and subsequent to World War II the Bundesbank); and

Bank of Spain, 1856. Today every modern nation has found it necessary to establish a central bank to assist in the control of money.

As discussed in the chapter on currency, the United States had two central banks prior to the creation of the Federal Reserve System in 1913. The firm, deep-seated opinions about the control of money resulted in a struggle within the political arena of the nation. Some considered banks and bankers to be evil, selfish and greedy and thus unfit to control the supply of money, and almost everyone believed that it was much better for the nation for the government not to be in sole control of the money. Private enterprise was championed as a better control of money and credit than the politicians of the day. Thus, there was fear both of control by private interests and by government. All agreed on the necessity for a stable currency and a steady rein on the circulation of currency. Hammering out a compromise for a central bank occupied the time and energies of bankers, politicians and economists for many years.

Following the National Bank Act of 1863 a degree of stability prevailed in the world of money in the United States. However, the country continued to suffer from periodic crises of currency shortages and money panics. Politicians blamed the bankers and the bankers blamed the government for interfering. The structure of the banking system probably was more to blame than any group of people. Under the national banking system a pattern of correspondent relations was established. Also, the nation was primarily an agricultural nation with seasonal demand for credit and currency highly dependent on the seasonal pattern of planting and harvesting of crops. As the harvest was completed, banks in the country areas had surplus funds. Being prudent investors, they sent these funds to their correspondent bank in the money centers — primarily New York — where they earned interest. When the next planting season rolled around, the country banks experienced a surge in loan demand and in turn requested the return of their funds from the money centers. This worked fine as long as the money center banks could return the funds promptly. However, being prudent bankers, also, they loaned the funds out to investors, frequently brokers in the stock market. In order to obtain the funds it was necessary to "call" these loans. Brokers, in order to repay the loans often had to liquidate some of their stocks. A flurry of "sell" orders could send the market into a tailspin and sometimes the money center banks were not able to collect the needed money to return to their country cousins. When this happened, the country bankers could not supply the needs of their customers and a money "panic" ensued. Script was called into use as attempts were made to meet the needs of day-to-day transactions.

The Use of Gold and Silver

The growing importance of controlled money and the power that accompanies it were graphically displayed during the period from 1870 to the passage of the Federal Reserve Act in 1913. The westward push of settlements into the mountain states of the United States brought with it the discovery of gold and silver in heretofore unknown quantities. The gold rush of 1858 and the subsequent discovery of silver lodes in the area now comprising Utah, New Mexico, Nevada and Colorado spurred development of the area. As production of the metals increased so did the political effort to make silver a partner with gold as a basis for the monetary system. Gold was, and has been for centuries a symbol of wealth and power as well as a basis for a money system. So the advocates of silver did not wish to replace this metal but argued vehemently for a place alongside gold for their metal. In many respects, silver was as good as gold as a monetary base. It was relatively scarce, did not deteriorate with time and could be accurately weighed.

After years of promotion and effective politicking, Congress passed the Bland-Allison Act in 1878. Known more often as the Silver Purchase Act, it provided that the United States Treasury would buy not less than $2 million and not more than $4 million worth of silver each month at market prices. The metal was to be minted into coin and/or used to back currency. Thus, this amount of money was being inserted into the economy each month. In effect, the Treasury was placed in the position of a central bank. During the period 1879–1882 the Treasury found itself with a surplus of funds and the only way to reduce the balances of the Treasury was to buy back government securities. This was done even though the additional funds were not needed by businesses at the time. A mild recession occurred in 1884 and although the Treasury had a surplus, it did nothing unusual to meet the situation. The recession did cause a shortage of currency in the New York area and the New York Clearing House Association issued $20 million in clearing house certificates to meet the liquidity situation. The action was suitable to the problem and the crisis soon passed. This illustrated that action could be taken by a private group which is similar to action that would have been taken by a central bank.

Purchases of silver under the Bland-Allison Act caused the Treasury to continue running surpluses. During the next several years the prosilverites and the more conservative politicians and bankers engaged in a heated battle over the question of the use of silver as a base for the money system of the country. Western states and most southern states supported the continued purchases of silver. The then secretary of the treasury, Daniel Manning, became so concerned about the continuing surpluses of the Treasury and the necessity of buying back government securities that he wrote "The Treasury's proper business as a fiscal is to receive the people's revenue from taxes in good money which it has coined for them and to spend that money as Congress bids, keeping no surplus at all beyond what insures punctual payments. A Treasury surplus is standing proof of bad finance — bad laws, if such have made it necessary."

In late 1884 Congress debated a resolution to prevent the suspension of silver coinage. Nathaniel Hill of Colorado, a pro-silver man, argued that the quantity of gold was inadequate and that silver purchases should be continued.

"There is no inflation of the currency, and it is contraction rather than inflation which is now threatened," he concluded.

The depth of conviction and emotion of the issue is illustrated by the following exchange of views on the floor of the Senate in the late 1880s:

> John Sherman, former Secretary of the Treasury and then Senator from Ohio: "At current market prices the silver dollar would have to be increased to 470 or 480 grains [from 412 ½] to achieve a bullion value equal to the gold dollar. If this change were not made the monetary system might revert to a silver base; and this kind of debilitation would separate us from the great, powerful Christian, intelligent, and civilized nations of the world in our financial operations."
>
> Senator John Williams of Kentucky responded, "What is there to prevent the bankers and moneyed men of the world, in other words, the goldbugs, from . . . requiring still more silver to be put into the dollar? We believe the fixed purpose of the men who advocate a monometallic system is to discredit silver altogether and drive it out of coinage of the world."
>
> Sherman retorted: "I wish I could cure my friend from Kentucky of the idea that the bankers or businessmen, or moneyed men of the world have the power to do what he supposes. The values of gold and silver are determined in the market place and market values are mysterious qualities made up by a combination of circumstances, no man can tell how or when . . . The market value of gold and silver will seek its level . . . and the money kings are as weak as King Canute in resisting the tide."

Two acts by the Congress are significant in the demise of silver as a base for currency. On July 14, 1890, President Harrison signed the bill that reduced the requirement that so much silver be purchased each month and substituted a flexible rule that called for purchases but not of a specified amount. Also, the amount purchased was to be used as collateral to the issue of silver certificates redeemable in silver coin.

Following months of debate and filibustering the Congress passed and sent to President Cleveland a bill repealing the silver purchase clause of the 1890 act. This in effect ended the use of silver as a base for currency. The presidential campaign that followed in 1896 brought the fact to the forefront as Bryan and McKinley sought the presidency. Bryan's famous "Cross of Gold" speech during this campaign made history but the die had already been cast and by the time of Bryan's speech mankind had already been "crucified on a cross of gold."

We have gone to considerable length to review the events of this period in our history to emphasize the importance of controlled money in our modern financial world. Coin, currency, and even checkbook money and credit cards assume a lesser role in the monetary world of controlled money. The institutions of state control to a varying degree the availability and cost of money and credit.

Momentum Toward a Central Bank

At the turn of the century events were cascading towards a major change in the monetary system of the United States. Two sticky problems remained in the monetary system: (1) an inelastic currency was unable to meet the demands for change in the need for currency, and (2) there was no lender of last resort for the discounting of commercial paper by banks. Also presenting problems were the circuitous routing of checks in the check-collection process and the lack of uniformity in the supervision of banks. The major political problem was who would control the institution or agency or group that would provide an answer to these questions. Basic principles that needed to be implemented had been stated by leaders in the political and business arena many years earlier. England and most European countries had resolved these problems to their satisfaction, or at least they had working solutions for them.

It was during the early years of the century that economists began to play a role in the development of monetary policies. Two names would be prominent in the early efforts to resolve the problems mentioned: J. Lawrence Laughlin, active with the American Bankers Association, and H. Parker Willis, special advisor to the chairman of the House Banking and Currency Committee. Later, Carter Glass would become prominent in the events of the next few years.

It was generally agreed that any central banking institution should not be under the control of the secretary of the treasury. Events of the past decades clearly reflected the inability of this office to be objective in administering policy. Mr. Laughlin stated this idea clearly as follows:

> We must establish some institution wholly free from politics or outside influence—as much respected for character and integrity as the Supreme Court—which shall be able to use government bonds or selected securities, as a basis for the issue of forms of lawful money which could be added to the reserves of the banks.... It is doubtful if a great central bank—apart from its political impossibility—would accomplish the desired end.

Most other economists preferred a kind of institution that used commercial paper as the vehicle for effectuating policy rather than government securities.

In the spring of 1908 Congress passed the Aldrich-Vreeland Act, which among other things called for a voluntary grouping of ten or more national banks into an association that would act as a clearinghouse for participating banks. This would be similar to the manner that local clearinghouse associations were already operating. They would have the power to issue notes with maturities not to exceed four months, and they would be assigned to different sections of the country as needed. The issuing of notes would be under the discretion of the Secretary of the Treasury, which was not considered a desirable feature.

The bill passed rather easily but some of the comments by congressmen are interesting. Carter Glass, from Virginia, objected on the grounds that the Treasury should not be involved. Testifying before the Banking and Currency Committee, James B. Forgan of Illinois, and then president of the American Bankers Association said ". . . the issue of anything that could bear such an infernal name as emergency currency puts the Federal government in the picayune and incongruous business of discounting commercial paper."

Congressman McHenry of Pennsylvania commented "the bill enables Wall Street to turn panics off and on at will. The secretary of the treasury would become the 'hired man' of Wall Street. Shall we close, as a fitting climax to this billion-dollar Republican Congress, by crowning our masters, King Morgan and King Rockefeller, the heroes of the last panic, or shall it be King Taft, Wall Street's hired man?"

Theodore Burton of Ohio favored the bill but wanted a more comprehensive measure. "The time is coming," he stated, "when that general principle of currency issue commensurate with business volume is going to be adopted either through a central bank or by other means."

Less controversial but perhaps of greater importance was a feature of the Aldrich-Vreeland Act creating a National Monetary Commission. This commission was co-chaired by Aldrich and Vreeland. Fifteen other congressmen were members, with A. Piatt Andrews of Harvard University as special assistant. The commission supervised numerous studies of monetary institutions in the United States and Europe. The commission's report included twenty-four volumes, and the final volume included a summary of norms that Aldrich had drawn from the Commission's work. They stated the following principles for a central bank.

    1. It should not copy the central banking structures of European institutions without material modifications.

    2. The American institution should mobilize and centralize reserves.

    3. The means for maintaining the central bank's reserves should be its rate of discount.

    4. In a period of distress the central bank should follow the Bagehot principle of extending 'credit liberally to everyone whose solvency and condition entitles him to receive it.' At the same time, it should keep its discount rate high to encourage a gold flow.

    5. The gold reserve should be used to the extent necessary.

    6. The central bank should have a monopoly of note issues but be restrained by governmental rules.

    7. Its operations should be free of political influences.

The voluntary clearinghouse association called for in the Aldrich-Vreeland Act of 1908 never became a reality. Following the releases of the report of the Monetary Commission created by the bill, Senator Burton of Ohio introduced a bill calling for the organization of a National Reserve Association

(NRA). This association was to fill the need for a central bank. However, supporters went to great lengths to avoid giving it that name as there was much resistance to anything that resembled centralized power. Senator Burton said the association was a logical step in the development of the banking structure and that it would be run by bankers with the supervision of the government.

The structure of the association was to include a central administrative and advisory bureau in Washington and fifteen regional branches. It would have forty-six directors, including the secretaries of agriculture, commerce, labor and the treasury. Other directors would be recruited from the districts throughout the country. The plan had the support of the American Bankers Association and was moving through the Congress with reasonable speed until the presidential election of 1912.

The election of Woodrow Wilson as president with a Democratic majority in both houses of Congress changed the complexion of the administration completely. The Republicans had held the reins of government for fifty-two consecutive years except for terms of Cleveland, who was as conservative as the Republicans. Now with the Democrats in power, consideration of any bill that had been supported by the Republicans was out of the question.

The Creation of the Federal Reserve System

In the late summer of 1913, Congressman Carter Glass introduced a bill to create the Federal Reserve System. Glass, from Virginia, had held the post of chairman of the powerful House Committee on Banking and Currency for several years and had been active in discussions directed toward a solution of the problems of inelastic currency and other banking problems. Senator Robert Owen, Oklahoma, managed the bill in the Senate, hence the name Glass-Owen Act.

Under the proposed Federal Reserve System, there would be not less than eight nor more than twelve regional banks with a coordinating agency in Washington, i.e., the Federal Reserve Board. The Board was to be nonprofit. "No financial interest," claimed Glass, "can pervert or control the Board. It is an altruistic institution, a part of Government itself, representing the American people, with powers such as no man would dare misuse." One of the basic duties of the Reserve banks would be to discount "eligible" paper offered by member banks. This would provide a means of expanding the volume of currency when needed by the community and as the need diminished, the bills would have matured and thus the amount of currency would be reduced. One of the sticky items in the bill was the definition of "eligible." About the only thing that could be agreed on was that maturity must not be more than ninety days and it must be paper developed as a result of transactions in business and commerce.

During the debate on the number of regional banks, proposals were made for as few as three and as many as forty-eight — one for each state. One was out of the question as that would place all the power in Washington. Three or four would lead to one in each of the money centers of New York, Chicago, St. Louis and possibly San Francisco. That was unacceptable as it would continue the dominance of the "selfish bankers." A practical solution and one that eventually was included was proposed by John Shafroth of Colorado. His reasoning went like this: No bank should be more than a night's train ride from a Federal Reserve Bank. Thus, if a country bank ran into trouble because of a possible run on his bank, he could gather up his commercial paper with maturities of thirty, sixty, and ninety days, catch the train, be at the Federal Reserve Bank by morning, discount his notes and wire his bank that there was plenty of money to pay the depositors. To place Reserve banks more than a night's train ride from the member banks it served would make it impossible to meet one of the very needs for which it was designed. To Congressmen, twelve sounded like a satisfactory nonmonopolistic number.

The legislators felt that the term central bank could not be used in any of the legislation, as it was monopolistic and would likely be run by "bloodsucking bankers" who were given special privileges to soak the poor, keep interest rates high and conspire with Wall Street speculators to cause panics that were profitable to the speculators and to the bankers.

Congressman Glass, speaking in support of the bill and answering criticism of the Federal Reserve Board, said "it [the Board] is strictly a board of control . . . doing justice to the banks, but fairly and courageously representing the interest of the people . . . talk of political control [of the Board] is the expression of groundless conjecture."

As the bill moved through the Senate, Senator James Lewis of Illinois responded to one critic as follows: "What does my distinguished friend expect in a political government? The Senator [one who raised the criticism] is right. The bill is political, political to the extent that it voices the political ideas of the people of this country, political in that it expresses in legislation the platform of the [Democratic party] . . . All things must be guided, honorable sir. To some men each system must be entrusted."

Our friend with the overnight train ride idea, John Shafroth from Colorado, responded to the idea that the bill would be in "the hands of the people." "Our bill is framed upon the theory that this is a bank of banks for the purpose of preventing runs on banks . . . We have 25,000 people's banks now. What is the use of turning into another people's bank? Every national bank in the United States is a people's bank . . . You do not want to mix a bank of banks with a people's bank . . ."

One of the key provisions of the bill was the "bills only" provision. This required the Federal Reserve banks to only discount notes that had a maturity of not more than ninety days and that represented loans for the purpose of carrying on trade. The transaction behind the loan must be for the production, marketing or storing of goods.

This was called "eligible commercial paper." Late in the debate of the bill, someone raised the question of what is eligible. Up to that point congressmen had assumed it should be short term paper tied to commercial transactions. But how short? And how to define commercial? John Meeks of Massachusetts pointed out that he had asked more than a dozen men in the field of finance and none could agree on the definition. Senator Knute Nelson said he thought it would be easy to define eligibility. "Short time commercial paper which is liquid and collects itself [provides] a natural system of elasticity." This is essentially what went into the final version of the bill.

Another view that was debated at length was the question of whether or not a member bank had the right to discount notes, or the privilege. This was to be settled by a very close vote as being a privilege. But to this day commercial bankers argue the point.

As mentioned earlier there was no question in the minds of all congressmen but that any organization — whether a central bank or association — that would serve the needs of the country must not be operated by bankers. They did not like the idea of the government being in the driver's seat either. But between the two, they were more willing to settle for government supervision, but not by the secretary of the treasury. The question of the kind of reserve to be held against any note circulation or deposits was so universally answered with the word gold that the question never entered into the debate. How much (what percentage) would be required was debated and finally settled at 40 percent for notes and 35 percent for deposits.

The bill creating the Federal Reserve System finally passed and was signed by the president on December 23, 1913. The importance of this new "creature" — the Federal Reserve System — as it moved more and more into the center of money and credit policies of the United States is such that it warrants a brief outline of its structure and operating policies. These have been modified by experience and by congressional action over the seventy years of operation, but the basic structure remains. It is so deeply imbedded into the nation's economy and financial structure that it may well continue for as long as the nation exists.

Chapter Eight
The Federal Reserve System

Implementing the System

In accordance with the act, an organization committee was named to take the first steps in establishing the new system. This committee was composed of the Secretary of the Treasury, Secretary of Agriculture and the Comptroller of the Currency. Its task was to outline the Federal Reserve districts, designate the location of the banks and make their report to the newly formed Federal Reserve Board. Their decisions were subject only to the review of the Board.

In designing the Federal Reserve System, the "one night's train ride" prevailed as the country was divided into twelve Federal Reserve districts, each with its own Federal Reserve Bank. The map of the country with reserve districts outlined on it looks disjointed until the major rail lines are superimposed. For example, the Dallas office is on the main line of the Texas and Pacific Railroad which runs across northern Louisiana to Dallas, and then westward towards El Paso and on to southern New Mexico and the very southern tip of Arizona. The Minneapolis district follows the Great Northern Railroad across North Dakota and Montana. Congressman Shafroth's idea was well-taken and as long as the railroads were the main means of transportation, the division of the country with due regard to the main rail lines was excellent judgment and provided all member banks with adequate access to their Federal Reserve Bank. A few changes have been made in the ensuing seventy years as air and truck transportation overshadowed the railroads. For example, the lower part of Arizona has been transferred to the San Francisco district and southeastern Oklahoma has been shifted to the Kansas City district and is now served out of the Oklahoma City branch.

There was little doubt from the beginning as to the number of banks — the act said not more than twelve nor fewer than eight. Competition for the banks quickly dictated the maximum number. Many cities and the bankers in those cities campaigned vigorously for a Reserve Bank for their town. Not only was it desired for prestige, but from the bankers point of view it gave ready access to their Federal Reserve Bank. Also, in the early years of the system up to the 1960s, payment for checks sent out from the Reserve banks for collection had to be paid for with drafts on a bank located in the city where the Reserve Bank was located. This virtually required country banks to maintain balances with banks in the Reserve cities. From the Federal Reserve Bank's viewpoint, it permitted the drafts in payments for the checks to be collected the day they were received.

In addition to the twelve Reserve banks, branch offices were established in several districts. These have been designed to provide better service to the member banks. Each Reserve bank was authorized to open branches with the consent of the Federal Reserve Board. As of 1984, there are twenty-five branches. Here are the locations of the twelve Reserve banks and their branches with the date of establishment for the branches shown in parentheses. The twelve Reserve banks all opened for business on November 16, 1914. The New Orleans branch of the Atlanta Reserve Bank was the first branch in the system.

Atlanta Reserve Bank
1. New Orleans, La. (Sept. 10, 1915)
2. Birmingham, Ala. (Aug. 1, 1918)
3. Jacksonville, Fla. (Aug. 5, 1918)
4. Nashville, Tenn. (Oct. 21, 1919)
5. Miami, Fla. (Apr. 1, 1975)

Chicago Reserve Bank
1. Detroit, Mich. (Mar. 18, 1918)

Cleveland Reserve Bank
1. Cincinnati, Ohio (Jan. 10, 1918)
2. Pittsburgh, Pa. (Mar. 16, 1918)

Dallas Reserve Bank
1. El Paso, Texas (Jun. 17, 1918)
2. Houston, Texas (Aug. 4, 1919)
3. San Antonio, Texas (Jul. 5, 1927)

Kansas City Reserve Bank
1. Omaha, Neb. (Sept. 14, 1917)
2. Denver, Colo. (Jan. 14, 1918)
3. Oklahoma City, Okla. (Aug. 2, 1920)

Minneapolis Reserve Bank
1. Helena, Mont. (Feb. 1, 1921)

New York Reserve Bank
1. Buffalo, N.Y. (May 15, 1919)

Richmond Reserve Bank
1. Baltimore, Md. (Mar. 1, 1918)
2. Charlotte, N.C. (Dec. 1, 1927)

St. Louis Reserve Bank
1. Louisville, Ky. (Dec. 3, 1917)
2. Memphis, Tenn. (Sept. 3, 1918)
3. Little Rock, Ark. (Jan. 6, 1919)

San Francisco Reserve Bank
1. Seattle, Wash. (Sept. 19, 1917)
2. Portland, Ore. (Oct. 1, 1917)
3. Spokane, Wash. (Jul. 26, 1917) (Closed Oct. 1938)
4. Salt Lake City, Utah (Apr. 1, 1918)
5. Los Angeles, Calif. (Jan. 2, 1920)

The Federal Reserve Board

It was assumed from the beginning that the coordinating structure — the Federal Reserve Board — would be located in Washington, D.C. It was composed of seven persons, including the secretary of the treasury and the comptroller of the currency as ex-officio members. The other members were appointed by the president with the advice and consent of the Senate. Terms were for ten years with one member's term expiring every two years. There could not be more than one member from any one Federal Reserve district and due consideration was given to representation from commercial, industrial, and agricultural interests.

During the period from 1914 to 1984 Congress saw fit to modify the structure and purpose of the system. Structurally, the major change was made by the Banking Act of 1935. Terms of the members of the board were changed to fourteen years, with reappointment prohibited after serving a full term. The name of the governor was changed to chairman and that of the vice governor to vice-chairman. Also, the name of the board was changed to Board of Governors of the Federal Reserve System. Members of the board were still to be seven in number, but the Secretary of the Treasury and the Comptroller of the Currency were dropped. Governors were prohibited from holding any office, position or employment in any member bank for two years after holding a position on the board. This prohibition did not apply if the person had served a full term.

A significant change was made in 1933 when the Federal Open Market Committee was authorized. This committee is composed of the seven members of the Board of Governors, the president of the Federal Reserve Bank of New York and four other presidents of Federal Reserve banks on a rotating basis. The original act authorized Federal Reserve banks to buy and sell government securities. The act creating the Federal Open Market Committee centralized such action within one body for the twelve banks.

The Full Employment Act of 1946 thrust a new objective on the Federal Reserve System. This act called upon the system to conduct its activities so as to promote full employment in the nation and to smooth out the ups and downs of the business cycle, a rather unique task for the central bank. The Bank Holding Act of 1970 thrust another duty on the System: it now had to oversee the administration of this far-reaching act. Throughout the 1970s hearings and questions on this act required an undue amount of time of the members of the Board of Governors.

The system was designed from the beginning to be nonprofit, and many of its services to member banks were free of charge. The most universally used service was the collection of checks and the delivery of currency and coin to member banks. These two services occupied the time and energy of well over half of the employees in Federal Reserve banks and branches. In many ways this was in competition with commercial banks offering similar services but at a price, usually compensating balances. The Monetary Control Act of 1980 made sweeping changes in the financial structure of the nation. Among other things it required Federal Reserve banks to recover their costs of operating in most service areas including check collection, transporting of currency and coin, safekeeping of securities and wire transfers of money. In addition it brought all banks — national and state-chartered — savings and loan associations and credit unions under the umbrella of the Federal Reserve System. This did not include control of the institutions other than member banks, but it did make the services of the system available to them, including the making of loans.

How the Fed Controls Money

In an economy that depends heavily on the cost and availability of credit, the role of the central bank is critical. Its actions can stimulate the economy or it can choke off expansion and bring the economy to a screeching halt. In the spring of 1980 President Carter invoked credit controls and instructed the Federal Reserve System to sharply curtail the availability of credit. Within weeks, consumers slashed their use of credit cards, bank loans dried up and the atmosphere of the nation was one of "stop whatever you're doing." The move was supposed to slow the inflationary pressure. It worked so well that by mid–June the Federal Reserve relaxed its control; soon inflation was again a problem as the nation resumed normal operations.

"Fed watchers" are now an integral part of most financial institutions. Stock market analysts give prominent attention to the action or inaction of the Fed. So our discussion of controlled money must take a closer look at this creature of Congress.

How does the central bank (the Federal Reserve System) control money? Basically by influencing the cost and availability of credit. The issuing of currency, as we have mentioned, is only to meet the demands of business for currency. But the central bank's impact on the cost and availability of credit can change the attitude of business, consumers and industry towards using credit. Also, the central bank serves as a bank for the government. Checks written by the government are sent to the central bank where the government maintains an account for the payment of the checks. In some cases, the government actually borrows from the central bank. The central bank serves as "fiscal agent" for the government, issuing government securities, redeeming them and maintaining an orderly market for these securities. If necessary to complete a sale of an issue of government securities, the central bank will buy them from the Treasury and give credit to the government in its account with the central bank.

While issuing currency on demand from banks is only to meet customers' needs, a vital key to the power of the central bank is its authority to issue currency. For example, assume that the government issues a check for $1,000,000 in payment for a computer. The seller takes the check to his bank and receives credit in his account. The bank sends the check to the Federal Reserve Bank and the Fed says, "We will credit your account." But the bank replies, "We don't want credit, we want cash." Because the Fed has the authority to issue currency, it replies "Fine. Bring your truck and pick up your $1,000,000 in currency." If a Federal Reserve Bank runs low on currency it simply orders more printed and pledges the necessary security for the additional notes. Hence, the term "printing press" money.

Originally, the Federal Reserve banks were required to pledge collateral against the circulation of their notes, 40 percent in gold and 60 percent in government securities or customers notes (which they had taken from commercial banks as collateral against a loan to those banks). The percentage of gold required was reduced to 25 percent by an act of Congress on June 12, 1945, and all requirements for gold collateral were eliminated on March 3, 1965.

It is not our purpose to discuss all of the purposes and functions of the Federal Reserve Bank. But a discussion of the three tools of the Fed as it influences the cost and availability of credit is pertinent to our review of controlled money.

The first two tools are quite easily explained; the third is more elusive. The first is loaning money to commercial banks. By changing the rate of interest charged on a loan to a commercial bank, the Fed can encourage or discourage borrowing. When a loan is made, it puts money into the banking system and thereby increases the supply of funds available and, other things remaining the same, tends to lower the cost of money. This interest rate is called the "discount rate." It can be raised or lowered by each Federal Reserve Bank with the consent of the Federal Reserve Board. This loaning of money to banks is similar to the commercial bank loan money to you or us. If the interest rate is lower, we are more inclined to borrow; if higher, we may decide to delay our borrowing.

The second tool of the Fed is "reserve accounts." Each financial institution — a bank, a savings and loan association and a credit union — must maintain a "reserve balance" with the Fed (some small institutions are exempt). By raising or lowering the amount of this reserve balance, the Fed absorbs or releases funds from the banking system not unlike the minimum balance you and we must keep with our bank, except the financial institutions are required by law to maintain their reserve balance.

The third tool of the Fed is not as easily explained. It is the power to buy and sell government securities in the open market. There is nothing comparable in our relationship with our bank.

The Fed maintains a minute-by-minute contact with the market for government securities through several dealers in the New York market. If the Fed desires to make the cost and availability of credit easier, it can buy government securities from the dealers. It pays the dealer by issuing a check drawn on itself. The dealer takes the check to his bank, deposits it and receives credit in its reserve account or cash. Thus, funds are dumped into the financial market. The bank receiving the credit may not need it and may sell the excess to other financial institutions and in this way the new money is spread over the nation. By reversing the procedure, the Fed can absorb funds from the market and make credit more costly and less available.

Financing Deficit Spending

A discussion of the control of money and printing press money would not be complete without giving attention to the fact that governments sometimes spend more than they receive in taxes and other revenue. The difference is obtained by borrowing; the usual way of borrowing is to issue government securities. In the United States, the Department of the Treasury issues a variety of securities as it borrows funds to meet the deficit in its operations. The most common variable in these securities is in their maturity. For example, "Treasury Bills" mature in thirty, sixty, 180 or 364 days. "U.S. Notes" carry a maturity of up to five years. "Bonds" are for longer maturities extending to as long as thirty years.

With deficits of $100 billion and more annually and with a total debt of more than a trillion dollars, the task of selling enough securities to meet the needs of the Treasury is not an easy one. The securities are offered to the public and to foreign investors on a bid basis. That is, prospective lenders (buyers of the securities) bid for the securities and the Treasury accepts the lowest bids. Small investors usually may ask for a small amount at the average bid, making it unnecessary for them to be experts in the field of finance.

Suppose not enough buyers bid for the securities? This would be embarrassing to the government and make it very difficult to pay its bills. Enter the central bank. As an arm of government, one of the duties of the central bank is to make sure that enough buyers are available. If necessary, the central bank will buy them. Most of the time, it uses its third tool—buying securities in the open market—to make sure there are sufficient funds in the market so that financial institutions, insurance companies, corporations and other investors will "subscribe" to the issue of securities.

To the extent that the central bank has to make a net influx of money into the market, it creates "printing press" money. If investors other than the central bank, and without the central bank putting extra money in the market, buy the securities, the nation simply loans some of its resources to the government. But if the central bank has to "monetize" part of the borrowings of the government, it results in the creation of money that does not have any relation to production of wealth or the increase in the resources of the nation. In effect, the funds are created out of "thin air."

During the period from 1970 to 1982, the Federal Reserve banks increased their holdings of government securities by $76 billion, about 5 percent annually. Some of this increase was needed to provide funds for normal growth of the nation's economy, but not more than 2 or 3 percent each year should be needed for this reason. The balance is printing press money.

Its Modern Influence

A not uncommon item on the evening news in 1984 was the report of the Federal Reserve Board on the change in the money supply during the previous week. It was usually brief, such as "The Federal Reserve Board reported that M-1, the most common measure of the money supply, declined $2 billion during the past week. This was in line with expectations." Sometimes the news commentator might make further reference to the change if it was unusual or if it was contrary to market expectations. If by chance the Federal Reserve had changed the discount rate—the rate charged member banks for borrowing from the Fed—the news item probably would be several sentences longer.

What happened during the seventy years of the Federal Reserve System to make its actions or reports of interest to the general public and to warrant a place on prime-time news? Prior to the 1960s, most people outside the financial community hardly knew what the term money supply meant or what the discount rate was, or cared about either. Even in 1984 most listeners could not give a definition of the terms but they had learned through commentators, publications, and a variety of educational projects that these items were important in their everyday lives. What happened on the financial scene did impact on their ability to purchase a new car or a new house on terms acceptable to them. More and more people had investments in pension funds, or the stock market, or held bonds, and trends in interest rates was a real concern.

The Federal Reserve System, created in 1913, has become the central actor in any appraisal of trends in business and industry. It is accused of being the instigator of business booms and depressions. If the chairman of the Federal Reserve Board makes an off-hand comment that the Fed might tighten its rein on the money supply, the financial markets go into hysteria. It is almost so bad that if he changes brands of cigars, the stock market flinches. Speculation as to the action taken by a meeting of the Open Market Committee is the duty of every financial analyst and economist. The official report of action taken is delayed from four to six weeks after the meeting so that such action will not be a major influence in the market or enable the experts to capitalize on such intentions in monetary policy.

The Federal Reserve System has emerged as a powerful institution whose actions do impact on financial markets, business outlook, and investment decisions. The power to make credit cheap or expensive, readily available or hard to get gives the system extreme leverage in the financial markets. This influence spills over into the decisions of business and industrial leaders and in fact into world markets. It has grown from the beginning of a "bills only" policy that was supposed to be almost automatic in supplying currency and credit, to a system that is a vital factor in the market for government securities, agency securities and foreign exchange. Largely through its open market transactions in the government securities market it keeps a minute-by-minute watch over the trends in interest rates and credit demands. A simple telephone call to a securities broker can change the attitude as well as the capability of the banking community. Substantial purchases or sales of foreign exchange can influence attitudes world-wide. In concert with other industrial nations, the Federal Reserve System exerts influence on world exchange rates. Working with the World Bank and the International Monetary Fund, the Fed's impact is truly world-wide. The net effect of these actions is to change the amount of money — albeit our unseen money we call credit — available to the nation.

On what basis or by what formula are decisions made that have such a critical impact on business and consumers? Our story should begin with a comment about the men who are charged with making such decisions. Are they politicians? Economists? Bankers? Businessmen? Perhaps they are some of each. Most have been economists or have had extensive experience in business or banking. Remember from our earlier comments that the Federal Open Market Committee is the focal point of decision-making, so we must look at the seven members of the Board of Governors and the presidents of the twelve Federal Reserve banks.

Members of the Board of Governors are appointed by the president with the advice and consent of the Senate. Remember, they are appointed for a term of fourteen years and cannot be reappointed. They can be removed only for gross negligence. They are prohibited from being an officer of any financial institution and from owning any stock in such institutions. They cannot speculate in the stock or bond market. Every restriction is placed on them necessary to avoid a conflict of interest in their decisions. Salaries are not competitive with the private sector so a person accepting a place on the Board of Governors does so at a financial sacrifice and primarily out of a sense of responsibility. Most governors do not serve the full fourteen years of their term; they usually move on to other endeavors. Presidents of the Reserve banks are subject to similar restrictions although their salaries are more competitive with the private sector.

As a result of these qualifications, the persons charged with making decisions in monetary policy are as far as possible from a position of being able to benefit from their decisions. This helps them to be objective and to give high priority to the economic health of the country.

In connection with being objective a word needs to be said about the disposition of the earnings of Federal Reserve banks. The discussions surrounding the formation of a central bank were emphatic that it should be nonprofit. Also, the suggestion was made that Federal Reserve notes should be taxed. The Federal Reserve Act as passed does provide in Section Sixteen for an interest charge against Federal Reserve notes. However, this device has not been used, but net profits of Federal Reserve banks are paid to the general fund of the United States Treasury. Expenses of operating the banks and of the Board of Governors, a dividend (not to exceed 6 percent) on stock in Federal Reserve banks held by member banks, and a transfer to surplus of an amount to bring that account equal to paid in capital are deducted from earnings. The amount remaining is transferred to the general fund of the United States Treasury. In 1985, that amount was $17.798 billion. No profits of Federal Reserve banks accrue to any officer, director or employee beyond their approved salary and expense reimbursement.

The Decision-Making Process

With highly qualified and objective persons looking at the problems of the nation, what facts do they have? The Board of Governors and the Reserve banks have staffs of economists and statisticians who review reports from all sectors of the economy and provide the governors and the presidents with analyses and theories for their consideration. Prior to each meeting of the Open Market Committee, briefings are held and every aspect of trends and possible developments are discussed. At the meeting, staff members again present information and views for consideration.

Apart from this mountain of statistics and theories, each president of a Reserve bank has a board of directors of nine persons who are chosen from the major interests in his or her district. These directors represent business, industry, banking, agriculture, educational institutions and consumers. They also are restricted in the relationships they have with financial institutions (except bankers who are to represent their sector). In addition, branch offices of the Reserve banks have five or seven directors from different geographic areas and businesses. Meeting monthly — and sometimes more often — these persons feed information that may not yet be reflected in the statistics to the presidents of the banks. So at the meeting of the Open Market Committee there are nineteen persons (only twelve of whom can vote) as well-informed as to the conditions in the nation as it is possible to be. At the meeting they can draw on information as well as their own appraisal of the situation and the factors affecting the nation's economy. It's not perfect but it is an outstanding group of well-informed, serious and knowledgeable persons.

What alternatives do the Committee have as it struggles to draft a directive to the manager of the Open Market Operations for the next few weeks? The members know that whatever action is taken, the impact of that action may not be known for weeks, even months — some would say years. There is a lag as an action is absorbed by the economy. To make money too tight as the economy seems to be rushing ahead too fast may not slow the economy for months and the impact may occur just when the reverse action is needed. To wait too long to take restrictive measures can result in an overheated and inflationary economy. Also, the magnitude of an action can be misinterpreted by the market and cause an unwanted effect. On top of these uncertainties is the basic fact that the effect of various actions is not known precisely: an action taken a year ago can have a slightly different impact a year later. It is not an easy task to reach a decision, and some have called it an art, not a science.

Others have argued that only one or two factors should have any consideration at all.

Further complicating the decision-making process is the fact that it is not known what impact various developments will have on the economy. Does a change in the money supply always result in a corresponding change in the demand for goods? Or is the attitude of consumers more important? Does a change in interest rates for short-term loans always precede a similar change in the rate for home mortgages? And if so, after how long a period of time? These and many other unknowns emphasize the lack of precision in achieving the objectives stipulated by the directives of Congress to keep the economy moving.

Just to add to the confusion, what works this year may not work next year or five years or ten years from now. To illustrate, Nobel Prize winner Paul Samuelson gave little attention to the money supply in his textbook in the late 1940s. But thirty years later his revised edition of his textbook proclaims the importance of the money supply in emphatic terms. Whether or not he is correct in the modification of his view, it is a fact that the money supply is now given a prominent place in the deliberations of the framers of monetary policy. Much of this change may be due to the work and writings of Dr. Milton Friedman and the supporters of his monetarist theory. They would say that only the money supply is important in developing monetary policy: make the money supply grow at about a 3 percent annual rate and ignore other factors.

In and through all of this maze of possibilities and theories runs the veiled shadow of politics. After all, this is a democracy and what the people want they will eventually get through the action of the Congress. To operate contrary to the wishes of Congress invites its intervention and power. The Federal Reserve System is a creation of Congress and it can, at any time, modify or eliminate what it has created. Elimination is not an attractive option as it would then become the duty of the Congress to make these difficult and at times unpopular decisions on monetary policy. This they are not likely to do. However, this does not prevent them from exerting pressures on the system to obtain the objectives they see as important. Nor does it slow individual members of that body from heaping criticism on the persons operating the System. For many years former Representative Wright Patman of Texas took delight in vigorously criticizing the action of the system as members of the Board of Governors appeared before his House Committee on Banking. Yet, he was knowledgeable about economics and never attempted to force his ideas on the system. Other members of Congressional committees use hearings involving the Federal Reserve as a sounding board for their ideas or those of their constituents. This is part and parcel of our form of government and it has served our country well. It is a way of life for those involved in making public policy, but it does not make it any easier.

The Federal Open Market Committee, as it meets behind closed doors and comtemplates trends in the nation's business, has three options: (1) do nothing and let the market place determine direction; (2) take action that will make credit easier; and (3) take action that will make credit dearer. Within these last two options there is the question of degree. How much easier? How much tighter? And through what means, Open Market operations or a change in the discount rate? (From a practical standpoint action on the latter must initiate with the directors of the Reserve banks but their action must be approved by the Board of Governors. But, a decision to recommend a change begins with the president of the bank who has taken his cue from discussion at the meeting of the Open Market Committee.) Should the committee modify the structure of reserves required of member institutions? This action is within the jurisdiction of the Board of Governors, but again the picture of the nation reflected in the meeting of the Open Market Committee will have strong impact on such a decision.

The specific action taken by the committee will be shown in a directive to the manager of open market operations at the Federal Reserve Bank of New York where purchases and sales of United States government securities are executed on behalf of the twelve Reserve banks. The wording of this directive often conveys a tone that is important to the manager as well as the contents of the specific directive. While the manager is expected to contact the members of the committee if directions are not clear or a material change takes place in the market, the directive usually provides guidance for three to four weeks until the committee next meets. Here is an example from such a directive:

> The Committee seeks in the short run to maintain the existing degree of reserve restraint. The action is expected to be associated with growth of M2 and M3 at annual rates of around 8½ percent from September to December, consistent with the targets established for these aggregates for the year. Depending on evidence about the continuing strength of economic recovery and other factors bearing on the business and inflation outlook, somewhat greater restraint would be acceptable should the aggregates expand more rapidly. Lesser restraint might be acceptable in the context of a significant shortfall in the growth of the aggregates from current expectations.... The Chairman may call for Committee consultation if it appears to the manager for Domestic Operations that pursuit of the monetary objectives and related reserve paths during the period before the next meeting is likely to be associated with a federal funds rate persistently outside a range of six to ten percent.

The difficulty of being precise in the execution of monetary policy is evident from the wording of this directive. Without his attendance at the meeting at which this directive was hammered out, the manager would have difficulty in following its direction. However, having heard the discussion, he has a feel for the intent of the committee.

Actions of the Federal Reserve System are subject only to the review of Congress. The system was designed, as was pointed out in the debate on the founding of the system, so that it would be "independent of the U.S. Treasury, the president and the banking community." Strong feeling persisted that it must not be under the control of either the secretary of the treasury or the "selfish" bankers. Within this independence, the system must keep in mind that it is an instrument of the people through the Congress and that its obligation is to make decisions most beneficial to the nation — its business, industry and consumers. It cannot for long act contrary to the direction that the nation wishes to go. It is obligated to be objective and to be aware of the long-range impact of its action. In fact, it may in many instances be the "bad boy," insisting on action that in the short run seems against the wishes of the people. As an example, the fight to control inflation in the late 1970s and early 1980s meant that money and credit had to be made expensive and that interest rates needed to move into very high ground. This sharply curtailed expansion and the housing industry and persons wishing to purchase a house were hit very hard. Housing starts came to a screeching halt in many communities. The system was severely criticized. Pickets arrived at the Board of Governors building in Washington, D.C., and bomb threats were made against Reserve bank locations. Believing that this action (restraining credit) was imperative to the long-term stability of the nation's economy, the system held fast and brought the excessive inflation to a manageable level. It was not without its price, but hindsight shows it to be a more acceptable alternative to the inflation that threatened the very life-blood of the nation.

The development and execution of monetary policy must take into consideration the needs of the United States Treasury. It must stand ready to insure the success of Treasury borrowings in order that the credit and prestige of the nation be maintained. Even though to do so is contrary to the objectives of the system, it must fulfill this role. To do so often requires more stringent measures on the part of the system as it provides funds to the economy to insure the success of a Treasury bond issue and at the same time attempts to restrain undue expansion of credit. Cooperation between the Treasury and the system attempts to prevent divergence of actions, but at times there is no alternative as the Congress authorizes expenditures beyond the amount of income to the Treasury, forcing the Treasury to go to the market and borrow funds.

Chapter Nine
Money and the Law

Legal Tender Laws

Legal tender is currency or coin, which according to law, may be legally offered, and must be accepted, in payment of a debt or other obligation expressed in terms of money. This country, like other countries, has enacted laws which establish what money is legal tender, and these laws have their basis in the United States Constitution:

> Congress shall have power to coin Money and regulate the Value thereof, and of foreign Coin, and fix Standards of Weights and Measures. . . . To borrow money on the credit of the United States — Article I, Section 8, United States Constitution.

> No state shall enter into any Treaty, Alliance, or Confederation; grant letter of Marque and Reprisal; coin money; emit Bills of Credit; make any Thing but gold and silver Coin a Tender in payment of Debts; pass any Bill of Attainder, ex post facto Law or Law impairing the Obligation of Contracts, or grant any Title of Nobility — Article I, Section 10, United States Constitution.

Furthermore, the Constitution gives Congress the power to establish mints, assay offices, printing offices, and perform other activities incidental to carrying out its obligations of providing a national currency. We have already discussed at some length the controversy over the authority of the federal government to issue currency and various acts of Congress regarding the issuing of coins and currency and the establishment of banks. This chapter will deal with other aspects of legality frequently raised about money.

In 1873, an act of Congress (now codified in 31 U.S. Code 460) made minor coins legal tender for any amount not exceeding twenty-five cents in any one payment. An act of June 9, 1879 (now codified in 31 U.S. Code 459), made subsidiary silver coins of smaller denominations than $1 legal tender in sums not exceeding $10 in full payment of all dues public and private. Under the above laws, pennies and nickels were legal tender for debts not exceeding twenty-five cents, and dimes, quarters, and half-dollars were legal tender for debts not exceeding $10.

The most recent law dealing with legal tender is Section 102 of the Coinage Act of 1965 (79 Stat. 255, 31 U.S. Code 392), reenacting a similar provision in effect since 1933, which provides:

> All coins and currencies of the United States (including Federal Reserve notes and circulating notes of Federal Reserve banks and national banking associations), regardless of when coined or issued, shall be legal tender for all debts, public and private, public charges, taxes, duties, and dues.

The above-quoted provision clearly and definitely establishes the legal tender properties of our paper currency. All denominations now being issued bear the wording "This Note Is Legal Tender for All Debts, Public and Private." According to the quoted provision, the absence of such wording on any of the older issued notes in circulation as mentioned therein, does not affect their legal tender status.

It is not entirely clear, however, whether the 1965 amendment by implication has modified or repealed the provisions of the 1873 and 1879 acts imposing limitations on the use of coins as legal tender for debts. The 1965 statute makes all coins legal tender, but it does not expressly make all coins unlimited legal tender for debts. Rules of statutory interpretation indicate that the acts of 1873 and 1879 are still in force, and the 1965 act is in force. According to law, when one statute deals with a subject in general terms and another deals with part of the same subject in a more detailed way, if there is a conflict between the two the more specific statute will prevail, regardless of whether it was enacted before or after the general statute. Until the effects of the 1965 act on the earlier statutes are the subject of a decision by a court of competent jurisdiction, a definitive answer cannot be given.

The courts have also played a part in answering questions concerning legal tender, as seen in the following decisions.

The law does not require that coins tendered in payment of a debt or obligations be absolutely perfect, and a genuine coin of the United States not so worn, defaced, or mutilated but that its mint marks are plainly discernible, and not appreciably diminished in weight, is a legal tender for its original amount.

However, mutilated coins which will not be accepted at their face value at the Federal Reserve banks or branches or by the treasurer of the United States, are not good legal tender.

Also, it has been held that a person is justified in refusing to accept mutilated United States paper money in payment of a debt or obligation, where such notes are badly torn, portions missing, or very badly soiled, and where their further acceptance or redemption value is doubtful. This is for the reason that a person to whom mutilated money is presented is under no obligation to take upon himself the burden of applying for redemption or to assume the risk of failing to obtain it. In one decision the comment was made, "A note from which a portion has been removed is not good legal tender, for although paper money may be legal tender, there is no statute impressing that quality on a portion of such notes."

If a person is tendered money in payment of a debt or obligation which he suspects to be counterfeit, he is under no obligation to accept it. Only genuine money has legal tender properties.

Counterfeiting

Counterfeiting is one of the oldest crimes in history. Hebrew shekels and Roman coins of early England were counterfeited and at some periods in history it was considered treasonous and punishable by death. For example, an issue of paper currency by the colony of Delaware in 1746, which was printed by Benjamin Franklin, carried the legend: "To Counterfeit Is Death." The Confederate government, in an effort to discourage the widespread counterfeiting of its notes, established the death penalty for any Northerner who tried to pass such notes.

During the early colonial days some people stooped so low as to counterfeit wampum, a form of bead and shell work used by the Indians and colonists as money. Counterfeiters made imitations out of cheap glass and soon thereafter few people would accept wampum. Our continental currency issued during the American Revolution had difficulties in being accepted because of lack of backing in specie, and it became more worthless when the British began to counterfeit it in large amounts.

During the Civil War, it was estimated that one-third of the currency in circulation was counterfeit. At that time there were approximately 1,600 state banks designing and printing their own notes, and as each note carried a different design, it was most difficult to detect one of the 4,000 varieties of counterfeit notes from the 7,000 varieties of genuine notes.

The adoption of a national currency in 1863 failed to resolve the counterfeit problem as the national currency was also soon counterfeited and circulated so extensively it became necessary to take strong measures. Therefore, on July 5, 1865, under authority of Article I, Section 8, of the Constitution of the United States, the United States Secret Service was established as a division of the United States Treasury Department to suppress the widespread counterfeiting. Also as a deterrent to this crime, from the mid–1860s to 1917, the reverses of several issues of currency, particularly National Bank notes, carried an excerpt from United States laws dealing with counterfeiting and stating the penalties therefrom. The laws passed by Congress establishing the Secret Service have been amended from time to time to add other duties to its jurisdiction, including the principal mission today of providing security for the

GENUINE

(Genuine plate makes clear lines)

GENUINE PAPER CURRENCY LOOKS GOOD BECAUSE...

- IT IS made by experts.
- IT IS made on costly machines designed just for that purpose.
- IT IS printed from steel plates produced by expert engravers. Genuine engraved plates make clear lines.
- IT IS printed on distinctive paper.
- IT IS GOOD!

COUNTERFEIT

(Counterfeit plate makes broken lines)

COUNTERFEIT PAPER CURRENCY LOOKS BAD BECAUSE...

- IT IS usually a product of inferior workmanship.
- IT IS made with equipment designed for other purposes.
- IT IS printed from a plate which is made by a photo mechanical process, causing loss of detail.
- IT IS printed on paper which does not contain the distinctive red and blue fibers.
- IT IS BAD!

PREPARED BY
U.S. SECRET SERVICE

president of the United States. In addition to providing severe penalties for the crime of counterfeiting, federal laws also forbid anyone to possess or pass a counterfeit bill or coin, reproduce a bill or coin or to mutilate or alter a coin or piece of paper money. Anyone convicted of passing a counterfeit may be fined as much as $5,000 or imprisoned for up to fifteen years, or both (Title 18, Section 471, U.S. Code).

Pamphlets are available at the offices of the United States Secret Service providing information on how to detect counterfeit bills and coins and other interesting information and instructions. In general, the distinction between good and bad money is that on fake bills the portraits are dull and smudgy and the printing is uneven. On genuine money these details are sharp, clear-cut, and evidence excellent workmanship. Look for the red and blue fibers in the paper. Often counterfeiters attempt to copy these fibers by printing colored lines on the paper. Rubbing a bill on a piece of paper is not a good test. Ink can be rubbed off genuine as well as counterfeit notes. No two notes of the same kind, denomination, and series have the same serial number, a fact that can be important in detecting counterfeit notes, since counterfeiters usually make large batches of a particular note bearing the same serial number.

In May 1986 the United States Treasury announced an additional anti-counterfeiting deterrent. The decision to alter our national currency arose out of an acknowledgment of the advancing technology in color reproduction. Widespread access to sophisticated copy machines suggested to Treasury and Federal Reserve officials that response to this development was warranted. In announcing the forthcoming changes, the Treasury stressed that no major design or color change was contemplated and reassured the public that the move would not affect the value and negotiability of existing currency.

A security thread is the main change contemplated at this point. A clear, polyester thread will be incorporated into the paper. It will be arranged vertically through a narrow clear field on the notes and will be able to be seen by the human eye when held to a light source. Each denomination is expected to have a distinctly identifiable printed pattern on the thread. On all notes except the one dollar, the thread will be located between the left border of the face of the note and the Federal Reserve seal. On the one-dollar note, the thread will run between the Federal Reserve seal and George Washington's portrait. The thread, embedded in the paper used for U.S. currency, will only be able to be detected with transmitted light. Copiers use reflected light and are unable to reproduce the patterns on the thread.

Secondly, there will be microprinting on the face of the note. The words "United States of America" will be engraved repeatedly around the portrait on the face of the note. Few copiers now have the capability to accurately reproduce this kind of microprinting.

Opposite: A U.S. Secret Service illustration explaining how to detect counterfeit currency.

These new features are expected to deter the casual counterfeiter and complicate the task of the professional counterfeiter. Both the new and existing currency will circulate as legal tender. Over time, the old currency will be removed from circulation in the normal course of currency processing at the Federal Reserve banks and branches. Production of the new currency is scheduled to begin in about May 1987, and the first notes will enter circulation three to six months later.

If you are in doubt about the genuineness of a bill, consult an experienced money handler such as a bank teller. Included in the pamphlet "Know Your Money" issued by the Department of the Treasury, United States Secret Service, are the following highly important instructions about money:

If You Receive a Counterfeit Bill or Coin
1. Do not return it to the passer.
2. Delay the passer, if possible.
3. Telephone the police or United States Secret Service.
4. Note the passer's description, and the description of an accomplice, if applicable, and the license number of the vehicle used.
5. Write your initials and the date on the bill, and surrender the bill only to the police or United States Secret Service.

The following is also quoted from the pamphlet "Know Your Money," issued by the Department of the Treasury, United States Secret Service: (from Public Law 85-921)

> Printed reproductions of paper currency, checks, bonds, revenue stamps and securities of the United States and foreign governments are permissible for numismatic, educational, historical and newsworthy purposes, but not for general advertising purposes.
>
> However, there are two important printing restrictions. The illustrations of paper currency, checks or bonds must be in black and white and must be less than three-fourths or more than one and one-half times the size of the genuine obligations. Illustrations must appear in articles, books, journals, newspapers, magazines or albums, and no individual facsimiles of such obligations are permitted.
>
> The plates and negatives, including glossy prints of paper currency, postage and revenue stamps, bonds, and other obligations and securities, used in printing illustrations in publications must be destroyed after their final use for the purpose for which they were made.
>
> Motion picture films, microfilms and slides of currency can be made in color and black and white for projection on a screen or for telecasting.
>
> No prints or enlargements may be made from films unless they conform to the above restrictions.
>
> Photographs or printed illustrations of United States and foreign coins may be used for any purposes, including advertising. The same is true for motion picture films and slides of coins.

Found Money

Whether or not a person can keep as his own property money which he has found depends on the facts and circumstances involved in each particular case. Several states have enacted legislation which govern the disposition of mislaid, lost, and abandoned property. Some of these statutes are called treasure-trove laws and others lost property laws, or antiquities acts. However called, they generally outline the rights, liabilities, and duties of the finder and the owner when lost or abandoned property is found in that particular state. These statutory laws prevail in those states. Among many other things, some of the statutes require that before a finder can retain possession of a lost article or money he must make a diligent effort to locate the true owner, including advertising, in some instances.

In the absence of statutory law, the common law (decisions of courts) is followed in cases involving found money. Following are some well-established decisions concerning found money under certain conditions and circumstances.

Traditionally, treasure-trove is valuable property found concealed in the earth (or sea) or in a house or other private place, but not lying on the ground, and the owner of the discovered treasure being unknown. In this country, the law relating to treasure-trove has been merged into that of lost property, at least so far as respect to the rights of the finder. The general rule in this country, in the absence of legislation, is that the title to treasure-trove or lost property belongs to the finder against the whole world, except the true owner. Therefore, there will be no further discussion of treasure-trove.

Generally, money or other property voluntarily laid down and forgotten is not legally considered lost. As to property which has been mislaid, a finder acquires no right to its possession. The right of possession as against all except the true owner is in the owner or occupant of the premises where the property is discovered, since he has custody of the property and owes a duty to the owner as a gratuitous bailee, with respect thereto. Thus, where property is found by one person on the premises of another, and the circumstances are such as to indicate that the loser in seeking restitution will apply to the owner of the premises—for example, where money or goods may have been thoughtlessly left in a place of business, store, shop, or train—it seems that the proprietor of the premises is entitled to retain possession of the money or thing pending a search by him to discover the owner, or during such time as the owner may be considered to be engaged in trying to recover his property. In the case of goods or money which may have been thoughtlessly left in a place of business, it is not clear from the authorities as to just what lapse of time will establish the fact that the thing has been lost beyond any possibility of restitution to the true owner. On principle it would seem that an extended period of time considered in conjunction with the place of finding and other attendant circumstances should be deemed sufficient proof of impossibility of restoration in order to entitle the finder to demand possession against the proprietor of the place where the things were found.

Lost property is that which *unwittingly* passes out of the possession of the owner, the whereabouts of which he is not thereafter certain. Where articles or money are accidentally dropped in any public place, public thoroughfare, or street, they are lost in the legal sense.

A finder of a lost article, although he does not by such finding acquire an absolute property or ownership, has such a right as will enable him to retain possession and keep it against all the world but the rightful owner. It follows with respect to lost property, that is, property which the owner has parted with *accidentally,* and of which he does not at any time know the location, the finder has a right of possession superior to that of the owner or occupant of the premises where the property is found. As previously stated, the finder becomes the owner of lost property against everyone but the loser.

To justify the finder in appropriating money or other property to his own use, the circumstances must be such as to afford reasonable grounds for the belief that it has been voluntarily *abandoned* and is therefore lost property in the full legal sense of the term.

The owner of the soil or premises on which treasure-trove or other property, including money, evidently hidden and forgotten by an unknown owner, is found, acquires no title by virtue of his ownership of the land or premises. It has been held that workmen finding money which has been buried or secreted on the premises of their employers are entitled to its possession.

The finder of lost or mislaid property is entitled to have it identified and the ownership established. This is not only his right but his duty, and he can be liable in case of misdelivery. If the owner fails to establish such ownership, the finder is justified in refusing delivery. This can be most difficult when money is involved unless it is found in a purse or other container bearing identification, or where the exact denominations can be furnished or other circumstances acceptable to the finder.

Whether more than one person present at a finding are deemed joint finders is sometimes a difficult question, where the evidence shows that some of them saw the property before the others had a greater share of the work or other action of which the finding was an incident. All that can be safely said is that the courts have inclined in doubtful cases to regard the finding as joint and all persons present and to any degree participating as joint finders.

As a general rule, and in the absence of a statutory requirement or a promise of the owner to pay, the finder of mislaid or lost property is not entitled to a reward. This common law rule has been changed by statute in some jurisdictions which allow a reasonable percentage of the value of the money or other property to the finder as a reward for its return. In the absence of statutes, if the owner promises a reward, definite in its nature, and the finder returns the money, or other property, the owner is bound to pay the reward even though the name of the owner is known to the finder prior to the offer of the reward.

These are just a few of the multitude of legal questions that can arise when money is found. Where small amounts are involved any questions that arise can usually be settled without litigation. However, if sizable amounts are involved, and because of the variances of the laws of the states regarding found money, it is advisable to consult an attorney.

If the property you find is money, the taxes you pay will depend on the condition of the money and at what amount it will be redeemed by the United States Treasurer. The amount of taxes due is a matter that should be discussed with the Internal Revenue Service, your state taxing authorities, or a tax expert.

Chapter Ten
You and Your Money

Record-Keeping

Stories of early coins, theories of money and discussions of monetary theories are all very interesting. But what about my personal finances? How can I make ends meet? How can I make the most of my resources? I don't really care whether I use Federal Reserve notes, silver certificates, credit cards or checks to obtain the necessities of life and a few luxuries, and maybe even have some funds left over to invest. Disagreement on handling family finances is a major cause of divorce. Every family struggles with the question of priorities in spending the family income. So let's take a look at the family budget, including its preparation and role in effective management of our income.

First a word about records. It has been said that the shortest pencil is better than the longest memory. In the matter of family finances a written record is the first requirement for evaluating the situation. Most people have a written record of their income; if it is from wages, the employer usually pays by check and includes a "stub" that gives essential information including the gross pay, deductions for income tax, insurance and other benefits and the net pay. Keeping these stubs in a convenient place takes care of a record of income and the expenditures made on your behalf by your employer. Interest and dividend income is reported by the payer of such income. Keep these statements or stubs along with other income information. Money from capital gains should be carefully recorded, including all the necessary information as to dates and amounts for use in filing income tax reports. Gifts are usually not taxable but for planning purposes they should also be recorded. In other words, make a written record (or save a written record) of any income that comes to the family coffers.

Record all expenses. Ah! That's where the fun begins. You mean I have to record the cost of lunches? Parking? Groceries? Gasoline? Yes! If you are serious about managing your money such records are necessary — but only part of the time! A detailed record of expenses for one month usually will provide a good basis for estimating such expenses for the rest of the year. But it is impossible to know where your money goes if a detailed record is not kept periodically. But we have little use for the notebook that some people keep to record every penny spent every day of the year—it is not that productive in managing your money.

When a record of a month's expense has been accumulated, then it is time to classify them and begin an evaluation of where the money was spent. You may like to design your own form but the following is one way of doing this.

Regular Expenses:	*Per Month*
Rent (or mortgage payment)	$_____
Utilities	_____
Life Insurance (prorate for each month)	_____
Car Insurance (prorate for each month)	_____
Medical Insurance (include that deducted from your pay)	_____
Taxes and Home Owner's Insurance if not included in your mortgage payment	_____
Car Payment	_____
Other Debt Payments	_____
Baby Sitter	_____
Car Expense-including gas	_____
Total:	$_____

These expenses are generally fixed and are not subject to much modification. The following are more discretionary and have some flexibility.

Variable Expenses:	
Food, including eating out	$_____
Clothing	_____
Telephone	_____
Contributions*	_____
Entertainment (include cable TV)	_____
Allowances for children	_____
Gifts (don't forget to provide for birthdays, weddings, Christmas, etc.)	_____
Vacation (allot a monthly portion to the annual vacation)	_____
Total:	$_____

*In many families this will be a fixed amount as a specific portion of income is given to church or other charity.

Here's another form that may be easier for some to use:

	Average Past 6 Mos.	*Goal for Improvement*
Our Monthly Income (take-home pay)	$_____	$_____
Expenses:		
Gift to church or synagogue	_____	_____

House payment (including taxes, house insurance and utilities, or rent)	_____	_____
Child care (include babysitting)	_____	_____
Spent at the grocery store and other food costs	_____	_____
Monthly insurance costs (life, accident— not car)	_____	_____
Transportation (car payment, gas, insurance, etc.)	_____	_____
Installment Payments other than car	_____	_____
Medical expenses (including hospitalization premiums)	_____	_____
School supplies	_____	_____
Clothing (including laundry and cleaning)	_____	_____
Gifts	_____	_____
Savings	_____	_____
Entertainment	_____	_____
Miscellaneous	_____	_____
TOTAL	$_____	$_____

Date Prepared: _____

Now total all expenses, and hopefully they will not exceed your income. If they do, then begin with the variable expenses and see where cuts can be made. It is at this point that managing and planning begin. Most people find that they are spending more for some items than they expected. Perhaps an item that is not especially important just got out of hand. When provisions for holidays and vacation are included, it is obvious why such times are a time of stress instead of enjoyment. If income is primarily monthly then unless plans are made for accumulating funds for these special occasions, money must be borrowed or heavier-than-usual bills will accumulate and the budget will be strained while the bills are being paid. The important thing is to plan for these and not let them come as a surprise.

Budgeting Your Money

Many studies have been made to show what percentage of a family's income should be spent for different categories of expense: 30 percent for food, 35 percent for housing, 10 percent for entertainment, etc. It is impossible to tell any family how they should spend their money — it depends on each family's priorities. Some may give a high priority to entertainment and be willing to spend less on clothing or housing, and others may want to save to buy a boat or a place in the mountains, or to provide educational funds for children. Each family must determine what is most important to them. But, if you want to know what some people have spent or what some think you should spend, here are some percentages.

These percentages are for a family of four with an annual income of $20,000, or, $1,667 monthly. This is take-home pay.

Housing (including insurance, taxes, utilities)	30%
Food (includes household supplies)	18%
Clothing	10%
Transportation	6%
Medical	3%
Insurance (life and auto)	7%
Credit (charge accounts and credit cards)	15%
Savings (include children's education)	5%
Discretionary (some call this "walking around money")	6%

These figures are for the year 1981. By 1984, many families were spending as much as 50 percent on housing. This is high, and unless there is a good chance of incomes increasing quickly, it can put a severe strain on the family budget. If you want a more detailed picture of household expenses, here's a report from the United States Bureau of Labor Statistics for the years 1981–1982 giving data on a range of family incomes.

	Lowest	*Second*	*Third*	*Fourth*	*Highest*
Average Household	20%	20%	20%	20%	20%
Pre-Tax Income (annual)	$3,562	$9,417	$16,190	$24,253	$42,440
Average Weekly Expenditures:					
(for selected items)					
Food, total	$27.85	$39.52	$52.00	$65.85	$80.86
Food at home, total	20.59	28.92	35.27	44.50	50.49
Cereals and bakery products	2.73	3.73	4.51	5.60	6.35
Meats, poultry, fish and eggs	6.64	9.69	11.71	15.78	17.30
Dairy products	2.78	3.77	4.72	5.71	6.89
Fruits and vegetables	3.39	4.68	5.40	6.43	7.75
Other food at home	5.05	7.05	8.94	10.98	12.21
Food away from home	7.26	10.60	16.73	21.35	30.37
Alcoholic beverages	2.32	3.65	5.44	7.09	9.74
Tobacco products and smoking supplies	1.65	2.57	3.53	3.62	3.48
Personal care products and supplies	2.04	2.84	3.97	4.89	6.96
Nonprescription drugs and supplies	1.04	1.44	1.81	1.72	2.37
Housekeeping supplies	2.10	3.16	4.01	5.67	7.34
Energy, total	16.86	27.07	33.65	41.59	50.85
Electricity and natural gas	7.70	11.05	12.13	14.91	18.38
Fuel oil and other fuels	2.17	2.85	3.32	3.57	3.34
Gasoline, motor oil, additives	6.99	13.17	18.20	23.11	29.14

In some families the answer to the family budget is more income. If this is the case, then evaluate opportunities to bring in more money, such as a second job or a change of job. Ask children to earn some of their money?

Following is a list of several things you can do to save money on your food bill:

1. Stay out of stores as much as possible. You will nearly always find something to buy whether or not you need it.

2. Shop from a carefully prepared shopping list, and if it's not on your list, don't buy it.

3. *Plan* your luxury items, don't let them "just happen."

4. Don't shop for groceries just before a meal. You'll be surprised how less tempting those nonessential items are when you have a full stomach.

5. If you send another member of the household to the store, give him or her a list and the exact money needed for the items.

6. Spouses should shop together if possible. This will increase co-operation on the food budget.

7. If your budget permits, buy specials in amounts that will last several weeks. A freezer is a must if you buy ahead on perishables.

8. If you are on a very strict budget, shop only once every two weeks, or longer if you can. Again, every time you go to a store it will cost you money.

Now a word about those credit cards. They are one of our most useful inventions, permitting us to buy specials when cash isn't available. Vacations can be charged on them, Christmas shopping can be done without cash, and cash can be drawn on most of them. But they have been the financial downfall of thousands. If credit cards or charge accounts get you into trouble, cut up the cards and close the charge accounts; there's nothing like a cash basis for living within your income. Here are some danger signs in family finances prepared by Family Financial Counseling, a credit counseling group:

1. Do you use credit to buy many of the things you bought for cash last year?

2. Have you taken out loans to consolidate your debts, or asked for extensions on existing loans to reduce monthly payments?

3. Even though your standard of living has stayed the same, does your checkbook balance get lower by the month?

4. You used to pay most bills in full each month, but you now only pay the minimum amount due on your charge accounts.

5. Have you begun to receive repeated dunning notices from your creditors?

6. Have you been drawing on your savings to pay regular bills that you used to pay out of your monthly paycheck?

7. You've borrowed on your life insurance before, but this time are the chances of paying it back more remote?

8. Do you depend on extra income, such as overtime and dividends, to get you through to the end of the month?

If you answer yes to two or more of the above, you may be heading for trouble and need to take another look at your financial situation, or maybe even seek counseling from your banker, friend, or a professional counseling service.

Planning for the Future

Family finances are very personal. It has been said that the pocketbook is the most sensitive nerve in the body. In our modern society, money is the key to security—to assure that we can get enough to eat, to have shelter, to be clothed, to feed our children, to help others and to have some special times of enjoyment beyond the essentials of life. To a teenager who cannot have the things that his peers have, lack of money can be devastating to his or her morale and self-esteem. The items may be far from essential and even "crazy" in the eyes of adults, but to the boy or girl from thirteen to nineteen years of age, they are necessities. The Apostle Paul commented that "the love of money [or material things] is the root of all evil." It wasn't the money itself but the desire for more and more of the things money can buy that Paul considered evil.

Anything as important to our lives as money is deserving of careful consideration and planning. Evaluating our expenditures must take into consideration not only our immediate needs for food, clothing and shelter but goals for the future. No one knows the future, but we all must make plans for it. Someone once said we should plan as though we would live a thousand years, but live as though today was the last day of our lives.

Any prudent person will want to make some plans for the future. Planning—or goal setting—can be a game and it can challenge the best of our imagination, intuition and judgment. Every coach has a game plan and every general a battle plan, so why shouldn't you have a plan of action for your life?

The number one step in looking ahead is to decide where you want to go. What do you expect to achieve in life? To be a millionaire? Own your own business? Be tops in your profession? Is family more important to you than business or professional achievement? Want to travel? Educate your children? What will you do when you reach retirement age? Answers to these questions—and others you may think of—provide the parameters for your goals.

Today's lifestyles permit much more free time than was true only a few years ago, and hobbies are an excellent way to spend that time. They should involve activity that you truly enjoy, and at least one hobby should not require great physical strength. Ideally, your hobbies should include other members of the family; you will enjoy doing things together and sharing is more fun.

The next step is to find a time when you and your family can sit down and give some serious thought to planning for the future. One important question is where do you and your husband/wife want to go professionally? Consider whether or not you are in the profession that you want to engage in for the rest of your life. If not, what area do you want to move into? Will this require more education? A change of locations? In many families this question will need to be answered for both husband and wife. Potential income will be a consideration. The following will help you in your planning:

Financial Goals:

    Monthly Income Now $_____ Goal: $_____
    During the life of a surviving spouse: $_____
    For other survivors (children): $_____
    The last two items will require life and disability insurance planning.

Investment Goals:

    Residence: (be specific—how large? location? style?)

    _____

    _____

    Other real estate: (lake house, ranch, cabin in the mountains, vacation
               house at the seashore?) List in the order of priority:
               which do you want first?

    _____

    _____

    What about hobbies?
    Do you have any now? List them in order of preference, i.e., the one
    you like most first. _____

    Limitations on these such as expense, requiring more than normal
    physical skill, can they be shared with your family?

    _____

    Other hobbies that you would like to develop: _____

    Limitations on these: equipment needed, cost? instructions needed?

    _____

    _____

Resources Available to Achieve Your Goals:

    Professional skills: (include education, natural skills, etc.)

    _____

    _____

    Health: (any handicaps or limitations?)

    _____

    _____

Financial Resources:

Salary & Wages:	Estimated Monthly Income	How Long Will Income Be Paid?
_____	_____	_____
_____	_____	_____

Guaranteed Income:
(especially important if you are approaching retirement)

	Estimated Monthly Income	How Long Will Income Be Paid?
Pension	$_____	$_____
Social Security	$_____	$_____
Annuities	$_____	$_____
Dividends (source?)	$_____	$_____
Interest Income:	$_____	$_____
Other Income:	$_____	$_____
Totals	$_____	$_____

Now is the time to act on the goals you have set. Without action, all of the paper work will have been wasted. Working through the steps of setting goals and taking inventory of resources probably raised questions. Here are some ideas you may have overlooked: What are probable trends in inflation? What is the long-term outlook for your profession or business? What is the business outlook for your community? Is it growing or is it becoming stagnant? What activities have you planned that are not available in your community? What education do you need that cannot be obtained in your area? Is your profession or business declining in importance or is it a growing and prospering situation? Do you plan any changes in size of your family? Taking all of these things into consideration, list three actions you should take, in the order of their importance.

How soon should you make a careful review of these goals and actions? Probably at least within three years, or anytime your family situation changes or you change jobs. Once a year—New Year's may be an appropriate time— is not too often to make such a review. Decide on a date now, and mark it on your planning calendar.

Planning an Investment Portfolio

Most families will at some time in their early years want to begin an investment program. If your employer has a profit sharing or investment program it may be the most profitable place to put extra funds. Even small amounts invested regularly can build for a special purchase or for retirement. Here are some ideas; the scoring after each is on the basis of one to ten, with ten being the best.

IRA and Keogh Accounts Money placed in these accounts can be invested in many areas. Your banker or broker can help you decide on the best for your situation. Remember, the higher the return, the greater the risk. Accounts in banks, savings and loan associations and credit unions are guaranteed up to a certain amount ($100,000 as of 1986). Federal income taxes on most money placed in these accounts is deferred until it is withdrawn, presently from age 59½ to age 70½. Check with your banker for latest IRS rules. Notice that it is deferred, not eliminated. But most people will be in a lower tax bracket when they withdraw the money. These are retirement accounts, not savings accounts; withdrawing funds from them before age 59½ involves a heavy penalty. Do not put money here that you may want to use before reaching age 59½. Safety and yield will vary; availability two (until age 59½).

Money Market Accounts Financial institutions and most brokers offer accounts that pay a competitive rate in the market and permit some check-writing on the account. Again, those in banks, savings and loan associations and credit unions are insured. Some brokers' accounts carry insurance, but not by the United States government. These are a good place to place excess funds from checking accounts, but the funds would still be available any time. Safety: ten (if guaranteed); yield eight; availability ten.

Certificates of Deposit Guaranteed up to $100,000, rate varies with maturity and competition in the market. Safety ten; yield seven; availability nine.

Agency Securities Issued by agencies of the United States government, including the Federal Home Loan Bank, Farm Credit Association, FNMA, Federal Land Bank, and others. Securities are usually for one or two years and are auctioned. Not guaranteed by the United States government, and market is more limited than United States securities. Safety nine; yield eight; availability six.

Annuities Usually sold by life insurance companies; can be "life time," set number of years, or other variations. Safety ten; yield five; availability ten.

Commercial Bonds Obligations of commercial or industrial corporations; interest and principal payments would come ahead of dividends on stock. Safety five; yield nine; availability seven.

Common Stocks Offer most opportunity for large capital gains; some pay dividends that are competitive with other rates; risk of loss is highly dependent on stability of the firm; an exciting place to invest but subject to all the risks of the market. Safety three; yield zero to ten; availability ten.

Real Estate Also an opportunity for large capital gains if investment is in the right place at the right time; tends to be a fixed investment that may be difficult to liquidate on short notice. Other than buying a home, real estate should be considered a long-term investment and undertaken with considerable care. Safety seven; yield zero to ten; availability two.

The following are investments, the income from which is exempt from federal income tax.

HUD Securities These are issued by the Housing and Urban Development Corporation and are fully guaranteed by the "full faith and credit" of the United States government. Being tax exempt, the yield is lower than other fully guaranteed securities. They can be purchased through a broker or bank. Safety ten; yield eight; availability eight.

Municipal Securities Issued by city, school district, water district, and other entities that are created by the state or municipality. General obligation bonds carry the authority to tax to provide payment of interest and principal. Revenue bonds do not carry that authority but are paid from revenues from the project financed by the bonds. General obligation bonds are generally considered safer because of the authority to tax to provide payment. These securities are only as good as the issuing unit and great care should be exercised in purchasing these bonds. Safety one to ten; yield ten; availability seven.

All of this record-keeping and planning requires time and may seem unnecessary. If you are one of the persons who has an income equal to all of your needs and wants, forget the records but do some planning. A wasted resource offends society and is a mark of foolishness on the individual. Make your plans, work your plans, enjoy life and make money your servant, not your master.

Chapter Eleven
Conclusion

What Is Money?

A very simple definition of money is "Anything generally acceptable within a country for goods and services is money." *Webster's Dictionary* defines money as follows: "Money (from the Latin *moneta,* a mint)—stamped pieces of metal, or any paper notes, authorized by a government as a medium of exchange." The functions of money might be considered in four parts:

Medium of Exchange This thing which is generally acceptable and what we call money is used to purchase goods and services, and when it is used in that capacity, serves as a medium of exchange.

Standard of Value Money serves as a standard of value. It is a common medium through which to compare values of different articles or services.

Store of Value When you are paid for your services or goods, you may desire to save a part of what you receive. If you received payment in the form of perishables such as butter, milk, eggs, etc., it would be almost impossible to do so. But when you receive payment in the form of money, you can do so by depositing it in a bank or even hiding it in your sock.

Standard for Deferred Payment We buy a suit of clothes and ask the merchant to charge it. We promise to pay in thirty to sixty days, and in so doing we promise to pay the merchant the dollar value for the goods delivered to us. We promise the merchant a certain amount of money, which we expect to receive from our employer in return for our services.

Some Definitions of Money

Cheap Money A term used to describe a condition when the general price level is high. At such a time a relatively small quantity of goods and services exchanges for a relatively high quantity of money; hence, money is cheap, or its value low, compared with the value of goods and services. The term is also used to indicate low interest rates.

Coin A piece of metal or alloy identified by certain designs or marks and issued by the government.

Convertible Money Money which is redeemable in the standard money of the nation.

Currency Anything that serves as a medium of exchange, whether of general or limited acceptability. Hence, besides cash (paper money and coin), this term in its broadest sense also includes checks drawn on bank accounts, postal money orders, express checks, traveller's checks, and similar instruments which, while not enjoying the general acceptability of money because they usually require identification of maker or endorser, are nevertheless important media of exchange in the business world. Indeed it is by means of checks rather than money that most business transactions are carried out.

Dear Money A term used to describe a condition when the general price level is low. At such a time a relatively large quantity of goods and services exchanges for a relatively small quantity of money; hence, money is dear, or its value high compared with the value of goods and services. This term is also used to indicate high interest rates. (Dear Money is just the opposite of Cheap Money.) (Dear Money is also frequently referred to as *Tight Money*.)

Deposit Currency The proceeds of a bank loan which have been credited to a depositor's account and made subject to withdrawal by check. The effect of many such transactions is to supplement money (currency and coin) with check or deposit currency, and thereby greatly expand the amount of currency in circulation. Such deposits are sometimes called checkbook money.

Elastic Money Money the quantity of which can be increased or decreased as general economic conditions may require. In the United States Federal Reserve notes may be regarded as an elastic currency.

Fiat Money Inconvertible paper money in support of which there is no reserve of specie. Governments issuing such money usually give it the quality of full legal tender.

Fiduciary Money Money not fully secured by gold or silver. The meaning of the term is sometimes interpreted to include all money not fully secured by gold. Regarded thusly, all money in general circulation in the United States today is fiduciary money, sometimes called credit money.

Hard Money Metal coins in contrast to paper money, and a national money with relatively stable value both internally and in international exchange.

Irredeemable Money Any kind of money that cannot be exchanged for standard money. All money of the United States has been irredeemable since 1933. (Also called: Inconvertible money.)

Lawful Money In general, any kind of money which has the quality of Legal Tender.

Legal Tender Currency or coin, which according to law, may be legally offered, and must be accepted, in payment of a debt or other obligation expressed in terms of money.

Money in Circulation In the United States, coins and paper money circulating outside of the United States Treasury, Federal Reserve banks, and vaults of commercial banks.

Paper Money Documents issued by the government, or by governmental authority, to be used as money. Paper money may circulate by virtue of a government's mere fiat and nothing else; or it may represent metal coins or bullion, held in some depository, up to the full amount of the paper's stated value. Between these two extremes, paper money may be secured in numerous ways and to a varying extent.

Representative Money Money fully secured by gold or silver. Until 1968, silver certificates were the only representative money in general circulation in the United States. When the issuance of silver certificates was discontinued on June 24, 1968, and the outstanding certificates were no longer redeemable in silver, there was no representative money in general circulation in the United States. Occasionally the term is used to indicate any kind of money that is fully redeemable in gold or silver.

Soft Money Paper money in contrast to metallic currency (coin), and any National money which is subject to unusual fluctuations in value, both internally and in international exchange.

Stable Money Money that maintains a reasonably constant value in terms of the commodities and services which it will purchase.

Standard Coin A standard coin contains the actual value in metal stamped on it.

Till Money A relatively small reserve of money kept in the vaults of banks for the purpose of paying out such cash as demanded, sometimes referred to as vault cash.

Token Coin A token coin contains less actual value in metal than the value stamped on it. Most modern countries, including the United States, issue only token coins. The reason people are willing to take token coins (and paper dollars) is that they have confidence in their government.

Selected Expressions and Slang

Bank The practice of banking started in Venice toward the end of the Middle Ages. The Italian bankers sat on benches, out in the open marketplace to conduct their business. These benches, or *bancos* as they were then called in Italy, gave us the word bank.

Cartwheels A name given to silver dollars beginning around 1878.

Don't take any wooden nickels Some probably think this corny expression started in America, but it didn't. Several hundred years ago the city of Alexandria in Egypt issued coins made out of wood because of the lack of gold or silver for coining. Because of the lack of intrinsic value, people soon refused to accept them, and the saying started, "Don't take any wooden nickels."

Filthy lucre Means filthy money. Lucre derived from Latin word *lucrum*, meaning money. Found in Paul's epistle to Titus (Titus 1:7).

Millions for defense, but not one cent for tribute When John Adams became President in 1797, he was anxious to avoid war with France and sent three agents to that country to settle the difficulty. They were met finally by three French representatives who tried to frighten the Americans, and they demanded money as bribes for the directors. Charles Cotesworth Pinckney (1746–1825), leader of the American delegation, is said to have uttered the much-quoted phrase "Millions for defense, but not one cent for tribute." Another version gives his angered reply as "No, no, not a six pence." This famous slogan also was said to have been a diplomatic reply that started the war with the pirates of Tripoli during President Thomas Jefferson's administration.

Not worth a continental In 1775 the Continental Congress authorized the first issue of paper money to finance the American Revolution with the issue to be limited to $2 million. Soon, however, other issues were put out with neither gold nor silver to back them. Such currency became worthless and people wouldn't accept it. Some are said to have used it to paper rooms, which led to the term for worthlessness that has remained to this day.

Penny wise and pound foolish Economical in small matters, but wasteful in large ones.

Pin money In the early colonial days the straight pin was a rare commodity and was allowed on sale only on certain days. The ladies of the house would save their small coins for just this kind of purchase and in time the expression "pin money" was associated with small change as we use the term today.

Ten penny nail, twenty penny nail, etc. In the early colonial days, nails were a scarce, much-needed commodity, and widely used as money. Before a nail-making machine was invented in the late 1700s, nails were made by hand by the village blacksmith and valued in terms of pennies. Hence the terms ten penny nail, twenty penny nail, etc., that are still heard today as reminders of the days when nails were used as money.

Two bits, four bits, and *six bits* During the eighteenth century, the large Spanish dollars, known as pieces of eight, were among the most important coins used by the colonists. Their name came from the fact that each dollar was worth eight of the small Spanish coins known as "reales." One reale equaled 12 ½ ¢ and was also known as a bit. Thus originated the expressions of two bits, meaning a quarter of a dollar, four bits, meaning a half-dollar and six bits meaning seventy-five cents.

The following are some American slang expressions concerning money:
Buck A dollar bill, a coin dollar, or the sum of one dollar.
Century (C-Note) A hundred-dollar bill.
Five spot, fin, or fiver Various expressions for a five-dollar bill.

Grand (Big One) A thousand dollars.

Jack, Dough, Lettuce, Bread, Moolah, Kale These are just some of the slang words used in describing money.

Mad money Money to be used by a girl to pay her way home from a date in case she quarrels with her escort.

Money bags A rich person.

Money talks Money accomplishes almost anything. Started around 1900 and now commonly used.

Penny-pincher A very stingy person. Undue sparingness in the spending of money.

Ten spot or *Sawbuck* A ten-dollar bill. A sawbuck is a sawhorse consisting of two X-shaped ends joined by a connecting bar or bars. It is also slang for a U.S. ten-dollar bill; so-called from the resemblance of the Roman numeral X to the ends of a sawbuck.

That ain't hay Used to emphasize that a certain sum is not a small amount of money.

Thin dime Used to denote a lack of money, such as: "I have only one thin dime in my pocket."

Twenty (Double Sawbuck) A twenty-dollar bill.

Two cents worth When a person offers his opinion or advice, such as: "I want to add my two cents worth." Very commonly used.

Two spot A two-dollar bill.

Comments About Money

Money bewitches people. They fret for it, and they sweat for it. They devise most ingenious ways to get it, and most ingenious ways to get rid of it. Money is the only commodity that is good for nothing but to be gotten rid of. It will not feed you, clothe you, shelter you, or amuse you unless you spend it or invest it. It imparts value only in parting. People will do almost anything for money, and money will do almost anything for people. Money is a captivating, circulating, masquerading puzzle.

Ask an economist about money and you may be sorry. He will tell you that money is a medium of exchange, a standard of value, a store of value, and a standard of deferred payments. See what we mean! — Banking Journal

Money is like manure, of very little use except to be spread. — Francis Bacon

Put not your trust in money, but put your money in trust. — Oliver Wendell Holmes

It's good to have money and the things that money can buy, but it's good, too, to check up once in awhile and make sure that you haven't lost the things that money can't buy. — George Horace Lorimer

Ready money is Aladdin's lamp. —Lord Byron

The value of a dollar is to buy just things; a dollar goes on increasing in value with all the genius and all the virtue of the world. A dollar in a university is worth more than a dollar in a jail; in a temperate, schooled law-abiding community, than in some sink of crime, where dice, knives, and arsenic are in constant play. —Ralph Waldo Emerson

A fool and his money are soon parted. —Saying current since the sixteenth century.

Money never made a man happy yet, nor will it. There is nothing in its nature to produce happiness. The more a man has, the more he wants. Instead of its filling a vacuum, it makes one. If it satisfies one want, it doubles and trebles that want another way. That was a true proverb of the wise man, rely upon it: Better is little with the fear of the lord, than great treasures, and trouble therewith. —Benjamin Franklin

Money is a good servant but a poor master. —D. Bouhours

Money is not required to buy one necessity of the soul. —Henry David Thoreau

Money is the life blood of the nation. —Jonathan Swift

Money has little value to its possessor unless it also has value to others. —L. Stanford

The use of money is all the advantage there is in having it. —Benjamin Franklin

Oh, what a world of vile ill-favored faults looks handsome in three hundred pounds a year. —William Shakespeare, *Merry Wives of Windsor,* Act III, Scene IV

To despise money is to dethrone a king. —Sebastian R.N. Chamfort

There is a vast difference in one's respect for the man who has made himself, and the man who has made only his money. —Dinah Maria Mulock

If you would know the value of money, go and try to borrow some. —Benjamin Franklin, *Poor Richard's Almanac*

When I had money everyone called me brother. —Polish Proverb

When money speaks, the truth is silent. —Russian Proverb

The almighty dollar, that great object of universal devotion throughout our land, seems to have no genuine devotees in these peculiar villages. — Washington Irving, Creole Village (This appears to be the origin of the expression "Almighty Dollar")

The love of money is the root of all evil. — I Timothy 6:10

It is not money, as is sometimes said, but the love of money — the excessive, selfish, covetous love of money that is the root of all evil. — Nathaniel Hawthorne

Penny wise, pound foolish. — Robert Burton

A wise man should have money in his head, not in his heart. — Jonathan Swift

Appendices

Significant Dates in the History of U.S. Coinage

1792 Establishment of Philadelphia Mint. Special coinage of half dismes (how dime was then spelled).

1793 Coinage of first cents and half-cents (regular issues).

1794 Coinage of first half dimes, half-dollars and dollars.

1795 Coinage of eagle ($10 gold coin) and half eagle ($5 gold coin).

1796 Coinage of first dimes and quarters.

1836 Change from hand press to steam-operated coining press.

1840 Silver dollar has figure of Liberty seated, a design used on all silver coins thereafter (except for silver dollars) until 1891.

1849 Congress authorized coinage of a double eagle ($20 gold piece) and a gold dollar.

1851 With the discovery of gold in California, and a need for acceptable money there, some private firms began minting their own gold coins.

1851 Minting of silver three-cent pieces of almost paper thinness; soon dropped as impractical.

1854 Coinage of three-dollar gold piece. Authorized in act of 1853.

1854 Establishment of San Francisco Mint.

1856 Flying eagle (small cent) made of copper and nickel.

1857 Circulation of foreign coins prohibited; Spanish silver dollars ceased to be legal tender.

1859 First Indian-head cent.

1864 Bronze two-cent piece, the first coin to use the motto "In God We Trust."

1865 Three-cent piece of nickel, discontinued in 1890.

1866 First nickel five-cent piece (there were earlier silver half dimes).

1873 Coinage of trade dollars, slightly larger than standard silver dollars, intended for use in the China trade where they "competed" with the Mexican peso. Withdrawn from circulation in 1887 because they did not help Far East trade, but tended to circulate at home.

1875 Coinage of 20-cent piece, discontinued in 1878.

1883 First Liberty head nickels, almost immediately withdrawn because the reverse bore only a Roman letter V and counterfeiters plated them thinly with gold to pass them off as five-dollar coins. The next issue of the coin read "V cents."

1906 Establishment of Denver Mint.

1909 First "portrait coin," the Lincoln cent.

1913 First buffalo nickel issued.

1916 First minting of Liberty (full length) half-dollar.

1921 First minting of Liberty head silver dollar.

1932 Washington quarter issued.

1933 U.S. government went off gold standard, gold coins called in.
1938 Jefferson nickel issued.
1942 Silver (35%) nickel produced to save nickel, discontinued in 1945.
1943 Zinc-coated steel cent produced to save strategic copper and tin (only year minted).
1946 Roosevelt dime issued.
1948 Franklin half-dollar issued.
1964 Kennedy half-dollar issued.
1965 All silver eliminated in dimes and quarters and reduced in half-dollars.
1970 Act of 1970 eliminated all silver in half-dollars and dollars.
1971 Eisenhower dollar issued.
1979 Susan B. Anthony dollar issued.
1986 Gold and silver bullion coins issued.

Significant Dates in the History of U.S. Currency

1690 Bills of credit (in effect, mere promissory notes) — the first paper money in America and in the entire British Empire — were issued by the Massachusetts Colony. Other colonies followed by printing paper money of their own.

1775 Continental Congress authorized first issue of paper money, to be limited to $2 million. Soon several other issues were authorized and total in circulation exceeded reasonable needs. Rapid depreciation of value resulted.

1790–1861 Between 1790 and the Civil War no paper money was issued by the United States government. On several occasions during this period the Treasury issued small amounts of interest-bearing notes in denominations down to $50 but they were not intended to serve as currency. Until 1836 the larger part of paper currency in circulation consisted of issues of the First (1791–1811) and the Second (1816–1836) Bank of the United States, a private federal-chartered bank. Afterwards, notes issued by state-chartered private banks were the chief form of paper currency.

1861 The first paper money issued by the United States — non–interst-bearing Treasury notes issued in 1861 and 1862 known as demand notes and greenbacks.

1862 Congress provided for the issuance of United States notes, and they were substituted for demand notes, which were retired. This new issue was popularly referred to as legal tenders.

1863 National banking system established and national banks authorized to issue notes. Most currency in circulation between the Civil War and the First World War consisted of national bank notes.

1864 National Bank Act of 1863, amended in 1864 and 1865, placed a prohibitive tax on state bank notes, causing state banks to discontinue their issuance.

1865 First gold certificates issued on a limited basis and for a small amount. First issued for general circulation as authorized by an act of July 12, 1882, was the Series of 1882. Last issue was in 1928 and gold certificates continued in circulation until 1933.

1878 Treasury authorized to issue silver certificates against silver dollars held in the Treasury for their redemption. Later issues also backed by silver bullion. On June 24, 1968, the Treasury ceased redemption of silver certificates.

1890 Congress authorized issue of Treasury Notes of the United States, known as "Treasury Notes of 1890," and also as "coin notes" because they were redeemable on demand in either gold or silver coin at the discretion of the Secretary of the Treasury. They were also legal tender. Authority repealed in 1893 and issue was cancelled and retired.

1913 The Federal Reserve Act of 1913 creating the Federal Reserve System, authorized issuance of Federal Reserve Bank notes and Federal Reserve notes. Federal Reserve Bank notes issued by the twelve Federal Reserve banks under conditions similar to the issuance of national bank notes. Federal Reserve notes issued by the twelve Federal Reserve banks now comprise over 99 percent of our circulating currency.

1929 Paper currency in the United States changed to small size.

1933 United States government went off the gold standard. Illegal for private citizens to hold gold certificates. This ban was lifted in 1964.

1968 Treasurer discontinued redemption of silver certificates.

1976 The two-dollar bill was issued as various kinds of currency since 1862; the last printing was the 1963–1963A series United States note in May 1965. Again issued as a Federal Reserve note and put into circulation April 13, 1976 (Thomas Jefferson's birthday), whose likeness appears on the note. The new $2 note is being issued to effect an estimated savings of from $4 to $7 million per year in printing $1 notes. The Treasury hopes the new $2 bill will replace about half of the one-dollar bills in circulation.

Interesting Items Used as Money

Item	Country Where Used
Mats and bark cloth	Samoa
Whale's teeth	Fiji
Rats	Easter Island
Stones	island of Yap
Beads	many islands
Fish hooks made of shells; teeth of sperm whale; discs of coconut shells and sea shells strung on long cords of coconut fiber	Gilbert Island
Eggs	Nauru Island
Sleeping mats	Island of Ponape
Pigs	New Hebrides Islands
Feathers	Santa Cruz Islands
Shell discs (not polished)	Banks Islands
Dogs teeth	Solomon Islands
Yams	Trobriand Islands
Tambu (shell)	New Britain
Boar tusks	New Guinea
Rice	Philippines
Drums	Alor Islands
Bronze guns, beeswax, buffaloes	Borneo
Buffalo and oxen	Cambodia
Cowrie shells	Thailand and many nearby countries
Tin ingots and gold dust	Malaysia
Silver and lead	many countries
Tea	China and Mongolia
Coconuts	Car Nicobar
Reindeer and cattle	Asiatic Russia
Sheep, grain, straw, camels	Persian Gulf area
Iron	Sudan
Salt	many countries, especially Ethiopia
Goats and cattle	Kenya and other countries

Item	Country Where Used
Beads	many countries
Gin	Nigeria
Corn	many countries
Furs and blankets	many countries
Wampum	North America, especially American Indians
Snails	Paraguay
Cacao beans, coca leaves	South America

In the Pelew Islands the most valuable bead is called "brak." Next in value is "Mungugau," then, "kalebukub"; these are for royalty only. For common people the names are "kaldoir," "kluk," "adelobok," and "kaymon a kvae." Also, betel nuts and leaves, *Chama pacifica* shells, tortoise-shell discs (for women only), and tobacco (for men only) are used.

Source: Einzig, Paul. *Primitive Money*. Pergamon, 1966.

Money in Circulation
(In millions of dollars)

	1960	1970	1980	1986
Total	$32,869	$57,093	$137,234	$211,971

By Denomination:

	1960		1970		1980		1986	
coin	2,247	7.4%	6,281	11.0%	12,419	9.0%	16,064	7.6%
1's	1,533	4.7%	2,310	4.0%	3,499	2.5%	4,021	1.9%
5's	2,246	6.8%	3,161	5.5%	4,635	3.4%	5,500	2.6%
10's	6,691	20.0%	9,170	16.0%	11,924	8.7%	12,136	5.7%
20's	10,536	32.0%	18,581	32.5%	40,739	29.7%	57,928	27.3%
50's	2,815	8.6%	4,896	4.8%	13,731	10.0%	25,695	12.1%
100's	5,954	18.0%	12,084	21.2%	49,264	35.9%	89,561	42.3%

Source: Statistical Abstract of United States, 1984 and U.S. Treasury Quarterly Bulletin, Winter, 1987.

World Population and Currencies

Country	Population in Millions*	Capital	Currency	
Algeria	19.1	Algiers	A. Dinar	= 100 Centimes
Argentina	26.7	Buenos Aires	A. Peso	= 100 Centavos
Australia	14.7	Canberra	A. Dollar	= 100 Cents
Belgium	9.9	Brussels	B. Franc	= 100 Centimes
Brazil	118.7	Brasilia	Cruzeiro	= 100 Centavos
Canada	23.9	Ottawa	C. Dollar	= 100 Cents
Chile	11.1	Santiago	Chilean Peso	= 1,000 Escudos
Colombia	26.4	Bogotá	C. Peso	= 100 Centavos
Denmark	5.1	Copenhagen	D. Krone	= 100 Ore

Country	Population in Millions*	Capital	Currency	
Dominican Republic	5.4	Santo Domingo	D. Peso	= 100 Centavos
Ecuador	8.4	Quito	Sucre	= 100 Centavos
Egypt	41.0	Cairo	E. Pound	= 100 Piastres
France	53.5	Paris	Franc	= 100 Centimes
Germany (FR)	61.6	Bonn	Deutschmark	= 100 Pfennig
Greece	9.4	Athens	Drachma	= 100 Lepta
Hong Kong	4.7	Victoria	H.K. Dollar	= 100 Cents
India	663.6	Delhi	Rupee	= 100 Paise
Indonesia	148.5	Jakarta	Rupiah	= 100 Sen
Ireland, Rep. of	3.4	Dublin	Punt	= 100 Pence
Israel	3.9	Jerusalem	Shekel	= 100 New Agora
Italy	57.0	Rome	Lira	– –
Japan	116.8	Tokyo	Yen	– –
Kuwait	1.3	Kuwait	K. Dinar	= 1,000 Fils
Luxembourg	0.4	Luxembourg	L. Franc	= 100 Centimes
Malaysia	13.3	Kuala Lumpur	Ringgit	= 100 Cents
Mexico	69.4	Mexico City	M. Peso	= 100 Centavos
Netherlands	14.1	Amsterdam	Guilder	= 100 Cents
New Zealand	3.1	Wellington	N.Z. Dollar	= 100 Cents
Nigeria	74.6	Lagos	Naira	= 100 Kobo
Norway	4.1	Oslo	N. Krone	= 100 Ore
Peru	17.3	Lima	Sol	= 100 Centavos
Philippines	46.6	Manila	P. Peso	= 100 Centavos
Poland	35.6	Warsaw	Zloty	= 100 Groszy
Portugal	9.9	Lisbon	Escudo	= 100 Centavos
Saudi Arabia	8.1	Riyadh	Riyal	= 100 Halalas
Singapore	2.4	Singapore	S. Dollar	= 100 Cents
South Africa	28.5	Pretoria	Rand	= 100 Cents
South Korea	37.6	Seoul	Won	= 100 Jeon
Spain	37.4	Madrid	Peseta	= 100 Centimos
Sweden	8.3	Stockholm	Krona	= 100 Ore
Switzerland	6.4	Berne	S. Franc	= 100 Centimes
Thailand	46.5	Bangkok	Baht	= 100 Stangs
Turkey	45.4	Ankara	T. Lira	= 100 Kurus
United Kingdom	56.9	London	Pound	= 100 Pence
USA	220.1	Washington	Dollar	= 100 Cents
USSR	263.4	Moscow	Ruble	= 100 Kopecks
Venezuela	13.5	Caracas	Bolivar	– –
Yugoslavia	22.4	Belgrade	Y. Dinar	= 100 Paras

*Date of census may vary with country. Source: Encyclopedia Americana 1986 and International Encyclopedia of Population 1982.

The Federal Reserve System
Boundaries of Federal Reserve districts and their branch territories

April 1984

LEGEND

— Boundaries of Federal Reserve Districts

— Boundaries of Federal Reserve Branch
Territories

⚫ Board of Governors of the Federal Reserve
System

◉ Federal Reserve Bank Cities

• Federal Reserve Branch Cities

· Federal Reserve Bank Facility

Federal Reserve Banks, Branches, and Officers

City	Zip Code	Officers
Boston*	02106	Joseph A. Baute, *Chairman;* George N. Hatsopoulos, *Deputy Chairman;* Frank E. Morris, *President;* Robert W. Eisenmenger, *First Vice President*
New York*	10045	John Brademas, *Chairman;* Clifton R. Wharton, Jr., *Deputy Chairman;* E. Gerald Corrigan, *President;* Thomas M. Timlen, *First Vice President*
Buffalo	14240	Mary Ann Lambertsen, *Chairman;* John T. Keane, *Vice President in charge of branch*
Philadelphia	19105	Robert M. Landis, *Chairman;* Nevius M. Curtis, *Deputy Chairman;* Edward G. Boehne, *President;* Richard L. Smoot, *First Vice President*
Cleveland*	44101	William H. Knoell, *Chairman;* E. Mandell de Windt, *Deputy Chairman;* Karen N. Horn, *President;* William H. Hendricks, *First Vice President*
Cincinnati	45201	Robert E. Boni, *Chairman;* Charles A. Cerino, *Vice President in charge of branch*
Pittsburgh	15230	James E. Haas, *Chairman;* Harold J. Swart, *Vice President in charge of branch*
Richmond*	23219	Leroy T. Canoles, Jr., *Chairman;* Robert A. Georgine, *Deputy Chairman;* Robert P. Black, *President;* Jimmie R. Monhollon, *First Vice President*
Baltimore	21203	Robert L. Tate, *Chairman;* Robert D. McTeer, Jr., *Vice President in charge of branch*
Charlotte	28230	Wallace J. Jorgenson, *Chairman;* Albert D. Tinkelenberg, *Vice President in charge of branch*
Culpeper Communications and Records Center	22701	John G. Stoides, *Vice President in charge of branch*
Atlanta	30303	John H. Weitnauer, Jr., *Chairman;* Bradley Currey, Jr., *Deputy Chairman;* Robert P. Forrestal, *President;* Jack Guynn, *First Vice President;* Delmar Harrison, *Vice President in charge of branch*
Birmingham	35283	A.G. Trammell, *Chairman;* Fred R. Herr, *Vice President in charge of branch*
Jacksonville	32231	E. William Nash, Jr., *Chairman;* James D. Hawkins, *Vice President in charge of branch*
Miami	33152	Sue McCourt Cobb, *Chairman;* Patrick K. Barron, *Vice President in charge of branch*
Nashville	37203	Patsy R. Williams, *Chairman;* Jeffrey J. Wells, *Vice President in charge of branch*
New Orleans	70161	Sharon A. Perlis, *Chairman;* Henry H. Bourgaux, *Vice President in charge of branch*

*Additional offices of these Banks are located at Lewiston, Maine 04240; Windsor Locks, Connecticut 06096; Cranford, New Jersey 07016; Jericho, New York 11753; Utica at Oriskany, New York 13424; Columbus, Ohio 43216; Columbia, South Carolina 29210; Charleston, West Virginia 25311; Des Moines, Iowa 50306; Indianapolis, Indiana 46204; and Milwaukee, Wisconsin 53202.

City	Zip Code	Officers
Chicago*	60690	Robert J. Day, *Chairman;* Marcus Alexis, *Deputy Chairman;* Silas Keehn, *President;* Daniel M. Doyle, *First Vice President*
Detroit	48231	Robert E. Brewer, *Chairman;* Roby L.Sloan, *Vice President in charge of branch*
St. Louis	63166	W.L. Hadley Griffin, *Chairman;* Mary P. Holt, *Deputy Chairman;* Thomas C. Melzer, *President;* Joseph P. Garbarini, *First Vice President*
Little Rock	72203	Sheffield Nelson, *Chairman;* John F. Breen, *Vice President in charge of branch*
Louisville	40232	William C. Ballard, Jr., *Chairman;* James E. Conrad, *Vice President in charge of branch*
Memphis	38101	G. Rives Neblett, *Chairman;* Paul I. Black, Jr., *Vice President in charge of branch*
Minneapolis	55480	John B. Davis, Jr., *Chairman;* Michael W. Wright, *Deputy Chairman;* Gary H. Stern, *President;* Thomas E. Gainor, *First Vice President*
Helena	59601	Marcia S. Anderson, *Chairman;* Robert F. McNellis, *Vice President in charge of branch*
Kansas City	64198	Irvine O. Hockaday, Jr., *Chairman;* Robert G. Lueder, *Deputy Chairman;* Roger Guffey, *President;* Henry R. Czerwinski, *First Vice President*
Denver	80217	James E. Nielson, *Chairman;* Wayne W. Martin, *Vice President in charge of branch*
Oklahoma City	73125	Patience S. Latting, *Chairman;* William G. Evans, *Vice President in charge of branch*
Omaha	68102	Kenneth L. Morrison, *Chairman;* Robert D. Hamilton, *Vice President in charge of branch*
Dallas	75222	Robert D. Rogers, *Chairman;* Bobby R. Inman, *Deputy Chairman;* Robert H. Boykin, *President;* William H. Wallace, *First Vice President;* James L. Stull, *Vice President in charge of branch*
El Paso	79999	Peyton Yates, *Chairman;* Sammie C. Clay, *Vice President in charge of branch*
Houston	77252	Walter M. Mischer, Jr., *Chairman;* J.Z. Rowe, *Vice President in charge of branch*
San Antonio	78295	Ruben M. Garcia, *Chairman;* Thomas H. Robertson, *Vice President in charge of branch*
San Francisco	94120	Alan C. Furth, *Chairman;* Fred W. Andrew, *Deputy Chairman;* Robert T. Parry, *President;* Vacant, *First Vice President*
Los Angeles	90051	Richard C. Seaver, *Chairman;* Robert M. McGill, *Vice President in charge of branch*
Portland	97208	Paul E. Bragdon, *Chairman;* Angelo S. Carella, *Vice President in charge of branch*
Salt Lake City	84125	Don M. Wheeler, *Chairman;* E. Ronald Liggett, *Vice President in charge of branch*
Seattle	98124	John W. Ellis, *Chairman;* Gerald R. Kelly, *Vice President in charge of branch*

Board of Governors of the Federal Reserve System

United States Mint
Domestic Coinage Executed During Fiscal Year 1986

Denomination	Philadelphia	Denver	West Point	Total Value / Total Pieces
Dollars—Non-Silver	$0	$0	$0	$0 / 0
Subsidiary:				
Half-Dollars	$6,890,208	$7,767,573	$0	$ 14,657,782 / 29,315,564
Quarter-Dollars	$147,256,529	$111,232,002	$0	$258,488,531 / 1,033,954,127
Dimes	$62,417,447	$49,732,909	$0	$112,150,357 / 1,121,503,569
Total Subsidiary	$216,564,185	$168,732,485	$0	$385,296,670 / 2,184,773,260
Minor:				
Five-Cent Pieces	$29,340,913	$19,578,428	$0	$ 48,919,342 / 978,386,845
One-Cent Pieces	$46,645,992	$46,148,840	$1,500,000	$ 94,294,832 / 9,429,483,250
Total Minor	$75,986,905	$65,727,268	$1,500,000	$143,214,174 / 10,407,870,095
Total Domestic Coinage	$292,551,091	$234,459,754	$1,500,000	$528,510,845 / 12,592,643,355

Foreign Coinage: None

Source: Bureau of Mint

Loans and Securities for all commercial banks[1]

Billions of dollars; averages of Wednesday figures

Category		1985							1986				
		June	July	Aug.	Sept.	Oct.	Nov.	Dec.	Jan.	Feb.	Mar.	Apr.	May
							Seasonally adjusted						
1	**Total loans and securities**[2]	1,808.6	1,822.2	1,833.9	1,847.2	1,855.5	1,876.0	1,900.4	1,930.0	1,935.5	1,944.6	1,947.9	1,955.9
2	U.S. government securities	273.1	275.4	275.1	275.5	274.2	276.0	273.1	268.2	273.6	269.5	270.0	274.0
3	Other securities	147.2	148.5	150.7	153.6	157.3	163.3	177.6	192.5	188.1	183.3	182.1	181.9
4	Total loans and leases[2]	1,388.2	1,398.2	1,408.0	1,418.0	1,424.0	1,436.8	1,449.7	1,469.3	1,473.7	1,491.8	1,495.8	1,500.0
5	Commercial and industrial	487.6	488.5	489.7	492.1	492.7	495.7	499.5	502.1	502.4	506.1	507.8	506.5
6	Bankers acceptances held[3]	5.1	5.2	5.1	4.9	4.9	4.9	4.9	4.9	4.8	4.9	5.2	5.6
7	Other commercial and industrial	482.5	483.4	484.6	487.1	487.3	490.7	494.7	497.2	497.6	501.2	502.6	500.8
8	U.S. addressees[4]	473.3	474.4	475.6	478.3	479.4	482.4	486.0	488.0	488.4	491.3	492.7	490.4
9	Non-U.S. addressees[4]	9.2	9.0	9.0	8.8	8.4	8.3	8.7	9.3	9.2	9.9	9.8	10.5
10	Real estate	397.9	402.2	405.9	409.5	414.0	418.0	422.4	427.1	431.4	436.1	440.7	446.2
11	Individual	276.6	280.0	282.9	285.4	287.5	289.7	291.5	294.6	297.4	299.5	301.1	302.7
12	Security	40.4	40.9	39.0	39.7	39.2	39.8	40.1	44.1	43.4	50.3	47.9	46.3
13	Nonbank financial institutions	30.6	30.8	31.4	31.5	31.5	32.0	32.6	32.6	31.9	32.3	32.4	33.3
14	Agricultural	39.0	38.9	38.6	38.3	37.0	37.1	36.3	36.1	35.8	35.5	35.2	34.7
15	State and political subdivisions	47.5	47.9	48.8	48.8	49.3	50.0	52.8	60.5	60.3	60.2	59.8	59.5
16	Foreign banks	10.0	9.9	9.7	9.6	9.3	9.0	9.1	9.1	9.2	9.2	9.2	9.4
17	Foreign official institutions	6.6	6.5	6.2	6.5	6.6	6.7	6.9	7.0	7.0	6.8	5.3	5.1
18	Lease financing receivables	17.5	17.8	18.0	18.1	18.3	18.4	18.8	19.4	19.6	19.8	19.9	19.8
19	All other loans	34.4	34.8	37.7	38.5	38.0	40.3	39.6	36.6	35.3	35.9	36.7	36.6

Not seasonally adjusted

20	**Total loans and securities[2]**	1,810.1	1,819.0	1,826.9	1,845.4	1,851.8	1,875.7	1,912.6	1,934.8	1,932.4	1,944.1	1,950.5	1,955.1
21	U.S. government securities	274.5	275.2	273.4	274.1	270.3	273.7	271.0	267.7	275.0	273.2	274.0	275.3
22	Other securities	146.4	146.7	150.5	153.6	156.8	163.3	178.7	193.8	188.9	183.9	181.8	182.3
23	Total loans and leases[2]	1,389.2	1,397.0	1,402.9	1,417.7	1,424.7	1,438.7	1,462.9	1,473.3	1,468.5	1,487.1	1,494.7	1,497.5
24	Commercial and industrial	488.2	488.6	487.9	491.4	492.0	494.8	501.5	501.4	500.1	506.9	510.0	508.3
25	Bankers acceptances held[3]	5.1	5.2	5.0	4.8	4.8	5.0	5.2	4.9	4.7	5.0	5.2	5.5
26	Other commercial and industrial	483.2	483.3	482.8	486.6	487.2	489.7	496.4	496.5	495.4	501.9	504.9	502.8
27	U.S. addressees[4]	474.0	474.1	473.6	477.5	478.4	481.0	487.3	487.3	486.3	492.7	495.4	493.0
28	Non-U.S. addressees[4]	9.1	9.2	9.3	9.1	8.8	8.8	9.0	9.2	9.2	9.2	9.5	9.7
29	Real estate	397.6	402.1	406.1	410.5	415.2	419.2	423.3	427.3	430.6	434.9	439.5	445.1
30	Individual	275.3	279.2	283.2	286.7	289.0	291.0	294.8	297.0	296.3	296.8	298.6	300.8
31	Security	40.6	39.2	36.6	37.5	38.6	41.0	45.4	46.8	42.6	49.4	48.4	45.6
32	Nonbank financial institutions	30.6	30.9	31.6	31.7	31.1	32.1	33.4	32.9	31.3	31.7	32.2	33.1
33	Agricultural	39.5	39.7	39.5	39.2	38.5	37.2	36.0	35.4	34.9	34.6	34.5	34.6
34	State and political subdivisions	47.5	47.9	48.8	48.8	49.3	50.0	52.8	60.5	60.3	60.2	59.8	59.5
35	Foreign banks	9.7	9.9	9.4	9.7	9.5	9.3	9.5	9.3	9.3	9.1	9.0	9.1
36	Foreign official institutions	6.6	6.5	6.2	6.5	6.6	6.7	6.9	7.0	7.0	6.8	5.3	5.1
37	Lease financing receivables	17.6	17.8	17.9	18.1	18.2	18.3	18.8	19.6	19.8	19.8	19.9	19.8
38	All other loans	36.0	35.2	35.7	37.8	36.7	39.1	40.4	36.1	36.1	36.8	37.5	36.6

1. Data are prorated averages of Wednesday estimates for domestically chartered insured banks, based on weekly sample reports and quarterly universe reports. For foreign-related institutions, data are averages of month-end estimates based on weekly reports from large U.S. agencies and branches and quarterly reports from all U.S. agencies and branches, New York investment companies majority owned by foreign banks, and Edge Act corporations owned by domestically chartered and foreign banks.

2. Excludes loans to commercial banks in the United States.

3. Includes nonfinancial commercial paper held.

4. United States includes the 50 states and the District of Columbia.

NOTE: These data also appear in the Board's G.7 (407) release. Data have been revised because of new seasonal factors and benchmark adjustments. Back data are available from the Banking Section, Division of Research and Statistics, Mail Stop 66, Board of Governors of the Federal Reserve System, Washington, D.C. 20551.

Source: Federal Reserve Bulletin

Consumer installment credit total outstanding, and net change, seasonally adjusted
Millions of dollars

Holder, and type of credit	1984	1985	Aug.	Sept.	1985 Oct.	Nov.	Dec.	Jan.	Feb.	1986 Mar.	Apr.
					Amounts outstanding (end of period)						
1 Total	453,580	535,098	506,090	516,420	522,978	528,621	535,098	542,753	547,852	550,939	555,094
By major holder											
2 Commercial banks	209,158	240,796	230,644	233,545	235,364	238,620	240,796	243,256	244,761	245,172	247,735
3 Finance companies[2]	96,126	120,095	109,457	114,927	117,565	118,356	120,095	123,717	126,001	127,422	128,154
4 Credit unions	66,544	75,127	71,938	72,433	73,474	74,117	75,127	75,810	76,431	76,953	77,578
5 Retailers[3]	37,061	39,187	38,751	38,723	38,890	39,039	39,187	39,416	39,497	39,844	39,826
6 Savings institutions	40,330	55,555	51,115	52,656	53,509	54,307	55,555	56,290	57,048	57,573	58,024
7 Gasoline companies	4,361	4,337	4,185	4,136	4,176	4,182	4,337	4,264	4,114	3,975	3,777
By major type of credit											
8 Automobile	173,122	206,482	192,923	198,656	201,994	203,766	206,482	210,661	213,342	214,361	215,028
9 Commercial banks	83,900	92,764	90,234	90,784	91,402	92,127	92,764	93,489	93,828	93,377	92,956
10 Credit unions	28,614	30,577	29,775	29,556	29,904	30,166	30,577	30,855	31,107	31,320	31,574
11 Finance companies	54,663	73,391	64,071	69,201	71,415	71,996	73,391	76,410	78,310	79,416	80,111
12 Savings institutions	5,945	9,750	8,843	9,115	9,273	9,477	9,750	9,907	10,097	10,248	10,386
13 Revolving	98,514	118,296	112,373	113,850	115,218	117,050	118,296	119,682	120,724	122,131	123,445
14 Commercial banks	58,145	73,893	69,079	70,453	72,507	73,076	73,893	74,991	75,953	77,021	78,424
15 Retailers	33,064	34,560	34,330	34,264	34,382	34,486	34,560	34,770	34,843	35,188	35,170
16 Gasoline companies	4,361	4,337	4,185	4,136	4,176	4,182	4,337	4,264	4,114	3,975	3,777
17 Savings institutions	2,944	5,506	4,779	4,997	5,153	5,306	5,506	5,657	5,813	5,947	6,075
18 Mobile home	24,184	25,461	25,173	25,341	25,320	25,315	25,461	25,371	25,573	25,584	25,521
19 Commercial banks	9,623	9,578	9,608	9,662	9,596	9,584	9,578	9,457	9,566	9,348	9,272
20 Finance companies	9,161	9,116	9,114	9,092	9,089	9,057	9,116	9,125	9,161	9,327	9,286
21 Savings institutions	5,400	6,767	6,451	6,587	6,635	6,674	6,767	6,789	6,846	6,909	6,963
22 Other	157,760	184,859	175,621	178,573	180,446	182,490	184,859	187,039	188,212	188,863	191,100
23 Commercial banks	57,490	64,561	61,723	62,646	62,859	63,833	64,561	65,319	65,414	65,427	67,083
24 Finance companies	32,302	37,588	36,272	36,634	37,061	37,303	37,588	38,182	38,530	38,678	38,757
25 Credit unions	37,930	44,550	42,163	42,877	43,570	43,951	44,550	44,955	45,323	45,633	46,004
26 Retailers	3,997	4,627	4,421	4,459	4,508	4,553	4,627	4,646	4,653	4,656	4,656
27 Savings institutions	26,041	33,533	31,042	31,957	32,448	32,850	33,533	33,937	34,291	34,469	34,600

28		77,341	81,518	6,051	10,330	6,558	5,643	6,477	7,655	5,099	3,087	4,155
	Total											

Net change (during period)

		77,341	81,518	6,051	10,330	6,558	5,643	6,477	7,655	5,099	3,087	4,155
28	Total											
	By major holder											
29	Commercial banks	39,819	31,638	1,556	2,901	1,819	3,256	2,176	2,460	1,505	411	2,563
30	Finance companies[2]	9,961	23,969	1,959	5,470	2,638	791	1,739	3,622	2,284	1,421	732
31	Credit unions	13,456	8,583	492	495	1,041	643	1,010	683	621	522	625
32	Retailers[3]	2,900	2,126	328	-28	167	149	148	229	81	347	-18
33	Savings institutions	11,038	15,225	1,641	1,541	853	798	1,248	735	758	525	451
34	Gasoline companies	167	-24	75	-49	40	6	155	-73	-150	-139	-198
	By major type of credit											
35	Automobile	27,214	33,360	1,722	5,733	3,338	1,772	2,716	4,179	2,681	1,019	667
36	Commercial banks	16,352	8,864	-116	550	618	725	637	725	339	-451	-421
37	Credit unions	3,223	1,963	59	-219	348	262	411	278	252	213	254
38	Finance companies	4,576	18,728	1,485	5,130	2,214	581	1,395	3,019	1,900	1,106	695
39	Savings institutions	3,063	3,805	294	272	158	204	273	157	190	151	138
40	Revolving	20,145	19,782	1,469	1,477	1,368	1,832	1,246	1,386	1,042	1,407	1,314
41	Commercial banks	15,949	15,748	907	1,374	1,054	1,569	817	1,098	962	1,068	1,403
42	Retailers	2,512	1,496	265	-66	118	104	74	210	73	345	-18
43	Gasoline companies	167	-24	75	-49	40	6	155	-73	-150	-139	-198
44	Savings institutions	1,517	2,562	222	218	156	153	200	151	156	134	128
45	Mobile home	1,990	1,277	158	168	-21	-5	146	-90	202	11	-63
46	Commercial banks	-199	-45	32	54	-66	-12	-6	-121	109	-218	-76
47	Finance companies	544	-45	-27	-22	-3	-32	59	9	36	166	-41
48	Savings institutions	1,645	1,367	153	136	48	39	93	22	57	63	54
49	Other	27,992	27,099	2,702	2,952	1,873	2,044	2,369	2,180	1,173	651	2,237
50	Commercial banks	7,717	7,071	733	923	213	974	728	758	95	13	1,656
51	Finance companies	4,841	5,286	501	362	427	242	285	594	348	148	79
52	Credit unions	10,233	6,620	433	714	693	381	599	405	368	310	371
53	Retailers	388	630	63	38	49	45	74	19	7	3	0
54	Savings institutions	4,813	7,492	972	915	491	402	683	404	354	178	131

[1]The Board's series cover most short- and intermediate-term credit extended to individuals that is scheduled to be repaid (or has the option of repayment) in two or more installments.

[2]More detail for finance companies is available in the G.20 statistical release.

[3]Excludes 30-day charge credit held by travel and entertainment companies.

[4]All data have been revised.

Source: Federal Reserve Bulletin

Money stock, liquid assets, debt measures
Billions of dollars, averages of daily figures

Item[1]	1982 Dec.	1983 Dec.	1984 Dec.	1985 Dec.	Feb.	1986 Mar.	Apr.	May
				Seasonally adjusted				
1 M1	479.9	527.1	558.5	626.6	631.0	638.4	646.1	658.6
2 M2	1,952.6	2,186.0	2,373.8	2,565.8	2,576.6	2,591.2	2,620.9	2,647.0
3 M3	2,443.5	2,697.3	2,986.5	3,200.1	3,239.3	3,259.1	3,288.3	3,306.6
4 L	2,850.1	3,163.5	3,532.3	3,836.8	3,878.3	3,891.1	n.a.	n.a.
5 Debt	4,661.3	5,192.0	5,952.0	6,809.8	6,964.5	7,012.6	7,069.5	n.a.
M1 components								
6 Currency[2]	134.3	148.3	158.5	170.6	172.9	173.9	174.4	175.8
7 Travelers checks[3]	4.3	4.9	5.2	5.9	5.9	6.1	6.1	6.1
8 Demand deposits[4]	237.9	242.7	248.4	271.5	269.2	273.2	275.7	281.6
9 Other checkable deposits[5]	103.4	131.3	146.3	178.6	183.1	185.2	189.9	195.1
Nontransactions components								
10 In M2[6]	1,472.7	1,658.9	1,815.4	1,939.2	1,945.6	1,952.8	1,974.8	1,988.4
11 In M3 only[7]	490.9	511.3	612.7	634.3	662.7	667.9	667.3	659.6
Savings deposits[9]								
12 Commercial Banks	163.7	133.4	122.3	124.5	125.0	125.7	126.6	129.0
13 Thrift institutions	194.2	173.2	167.3	179.1	179.9	181.2	184.9	189.6
Small denomination time deposits[9]								
14 Commercial Banks	380.4	351.1	387.2	384.1	388.1	389.0	387.9	384.8
15 Thrift institutions	472.4	434.1	500.3	496.2	502.9	505.7	508.3	506.2
Money market mutual funds								
16 General purpose and broker/dealer	185.2	138.2	167.5	176.5	181.0	186.2	191.4	193.4
17 Institution-only	51.1	43.2	62.7	64.6	67.7	70.2	74.1	76.1
Large denomination time deposits[10]								
18 Commercial Banks[11]	262.1	228.7	263.7	279.1	291.5	287.0	287.0	281.4
19 Thrift institutions	65.8	101.1	150.2	157.3	159.7	163.4	165.0	164.7
Debt components								
20 Federal debt	979.2	1,173.0	1,367.3	1,586.3	1,621.1	1,628.2	1,638.8	n.a.
21 Non-federal debt	3,682.1	4,019.0	4,584.7	5,223.5	5,343.5	5,384.4	5,430.6	n.a.

					Not seasonally adj			
22	M1	490.9	538.8	570.5	639.9	619.9	630.5	652.8	651.7
23	M2	1,958.6	2,192.8	2,380.8	2,573.9	2,569.9	2,593.2	2,630.6	2,638.0
24	M3	2,453.3	2,707.9	2,997.9	3,212.8	3,231.3	3,259.4	3,294.8	3,299.8
25	L	2,856.4	3,170.1	3,537.5	3,843.1	3,870.7	3,895.3	n.a.	n.a.
26	Debt	4,655.7	5,186.5	5,946.2	6,803.9	6,945.2	6,985.6	7,040.9	n.a.
	M1 components								
27	Currency[2]	136.5	150.5	160.9	173.1	170.6	172.3	173.6	175.8
28	Travelers checks[3]	4.1	4.6	4.9	5.5	5.6	5.8	5.8	5.9
29	Demand deposits[4]	246.2	251.3	257.3	281.3	262.0	267.1	278.6	276.7
30	Other checkable deposits[5]	104.1	132.4	147.5	180.1	181.0	185.3	194.7	193.4
	Nontransactions components								
31	M2[6]	1,467.7	1,654.0	1,810.3	1,934.0	1,951.7	1,962.7	1,977.5	1,986.2
32	M3 only[7]	494.7	515.1	617.0	638.9	661.4	666.2	663.7	661.8
	Money market deposit accounts								
33	Commercial banks	26.3	230.5	267.2	332.4	337.0	340.3	344.7	348.5
34	Thrift institutions	16.9	148.7	149.7	179.6	179.4	180.2	180.4	182.1
	Savings deposits[8]								
35	Commercial Banks	162.1	132.2	121.4	123.5	123.6	124.9	127.2	129.5
36	Thrift institutions	193.1	172.3	166.5	178.3	179.1	181.6	185.8	190.4
	Small denomination time deposits[9]								
37	Commercial Banks	380.1	351.1	387.6	384.8	387.1	387.2	384.4	382.3
38	Thrift institutions	471.7	434.2	501.2	497.6	504.6	504.6	505.4	502.3
	Money market mutual funds								
39	General purpose and broker/dealer	185.2	138.2	167.5	176.5	181.0	186.2	191.4	193.4
40	Institution-only	51.1	43.2	62.7	64.6	67.7	70.2	74.1	76.1
	Large denomination time deposits[10]								
41	Commercial Banks	265.2	230.8	265.5	280.9	290.4	287.6	283.5	280.7
42	Thrift institutions	65.8	101.4	150.6	157.8	160.7	163.2	164.0	164.2
	Debt components								
43	Federal debt	976.4	1,170.2	1,364.7	1,583.7	1,621.0	1,633.3	1,644.6	n.a.
44	Non-federal debt	3,679.3	4,016.3	4,581.6	5,220.2	5,324.2	5,352.3	5,396.2	n.a.

Source: Federal Reserve Bulletin. For footnotes see page 154.

Notes to page 153

[1]Composition of the money stock measures and debt is as follows:

M1: (1) currency outside the Treasury, Federal Reserve Banks, and the vaults of commercial banks; (2) travelers checks of nonbank issuers; (3) demand deposits at all commercial banks other than those due to domestic banks, the U.S. government, and foreign banks and official institutions less cash items in the process of collection and Federal Reserve float; and (4) other checkable deposits (OCD) consisting of negotiable order of withdrawal (NOW) and automatic transfer service (ATS) accounts at depository institutions, credit union share draft accounts, and demand deposits at thrift institutions. The currency and demand deposit components exclude the estimated amount of vault cash and demand deposits respectively held by thrift institutions to service their OCD liabilities.

M2: M1 plus overnight (and continuing contract) repurchase agreements (RPs) issued by all commercial banks and overnight Eurodollars issued to U.S. residents by foreign branches of U.S. banks worldwide, MMDAs, savings and small-denomination time deposits (time deposits — including retail RPs — in amounts of less than $100,000), and balances in both taxable and tax-exempt general purpose and broker/dealer money market mutual funds. Excludes individual retirement accounts (IRA) and Keogh balances at depository institutions and money market funds. Also excludes all balances held by U.S. commercial banks, money market funds (general purpose and broker/dealer), foreign governments and commercial banks, and the U.S. government. Also subtracted is a consolidation adjustment that represents the estimated amount of demand deposits and vault cash held by thrift institutions to service their time and savings deposits.

M3: M2 plus large-denomination time deposits and term RP liabilities (in amounts of $100,000 or more) issued by commercial banks and thrift institutions, term Eurodollars held by U.S. residents at foreign branches of U.S. banks worldwide and at all banking offices in the United Kingdom and Canada, and balances in both taxable and tax-exempt, institution-only money market mutual funds. Excludes amounts held by depository institutions, the U.S. government, money market funds, and foreign banks and official institutions. Also subtracted is a consolidation adjustment that represents the estimated amount of overnight RPs and Eurodollars held by institution-only money market mutual funds.

L: M3 plus the nonbank public holdings of U.S. savings bonds, short-term Treasury securities, commercial paper and bankers acceptances, net of money market mutual fund holdings of these assets.

Debt: Debt of domestic nonfinancial sectors consists of outstanding credit market debt of the U.S. government, state and local governments, and private nonfinancial sectors. Private debt consists of corporate bonds, mortgages, consumer credit (including bank loans), other bank loans, commercial paper, bankers acceptances, and other debt instruments. The source of data on domestic nonfinancial debt is the Federal Reserve Board's flow of funds accounts. Debt data are based on monthly averages.

[2]Currency outside the U.S. Treasury, Federal Reserve Banks, and vaults of commercial banks. Excludes the estimated amount of vault cash held by thrift institutions to service their OCD liabilities.

[3]Outstanding amount of U.S. dollar-denominated travelers checks of non-bank issuers. Travelers checks issued by depository institutions are included in demand deposits.

[4]Demand deposits at commercial banks and foreign-related institutions other than those due to domestic banks, the U.S. government, and foreign banks and official institutions less cash items in the process of collection and Federal Reserve float.

Excludes the estimated amount of demand deposits held at commercial banks by thrift institutions to service their OCD liabilities.

[5]Consists of NOW and ATS balances at all depository institutions, credit union share draft balances, and demand deposits at thrift institutions. Other checkable deposits seasonally adjusted equals the difference between the seasonally adjusted sum of demand deposits plus OCD and seasonally adjusted demand deposits. Included are all ceiling free "Super NOWs," authorized by the Depository Institutions Deregulation committee to be offered beginning Jan. 5, 1983.

[6]Sum of overnight RPs and overnight Eurodollars, money market fund balances (general purpose and broker/dealer), MMDAs, and savings and small time deposits, less the consolidation adjustment that represents the estimated amount of demand deposits and vault cash held by thrift institutions to service their time and savings deposits liabilities.

[7]Sum of large time deposits, term RPs and term Eurodollars of U.S. residents, money market fund balances (institution-only), less a consolidation adjustment that represents the estimated amount of overnight RPs and Eurodollars held by institution-only money market funds.

[8]Savings deposits exclude MMDAs.

[9]Small-denomination time deposits—including retail RPs—are those issued in amounts of less than $100,000. All individual retirement accounts (IRA) and Keogh accounts at commercial banks and thrifts are subtracted from small time deposits.

[10]Large-denomination time deposits are those issued in amounts of $100,000 or more, excluding those booked at international banking facilities.

[11]Large-denomination time deposits at commercial banks less those held by money market mutual funds, depository institutions, and foreign banks and official institutions.

NOTE: Latest monthly and weekly figures are available from the Board's H.6 (508) release. Historical data are available from the Banking Section, Division of Research and Statistics, Board of Governors of the Federal Reserve System, Washington, D.C. 20551.

Gold and Silver Bullion Coin Specifications

One Ounce Gold Bullion Coin

Weight:	33.931 grams (1.091 troy ounces)
Diameter:	32.70 millimeters (1.287 inches)
Thickness (est):	2.91 millimeters (0.115 inches)
Content:	Gold 31.104 grams (1.000 troy ounces)
	Silver 1.018 grams (0.033 troy ounces)
	Copper 1.810 grams (0.058 troy ounces)

Half Ounce Gold Bullion Coin

Weight:	16.966 grams (0.5455 troy ounces)
Diameter:	27.00 millimeters (1.063 inches)
Thickness (est):	2.16 millimeters (0.085 inches)
Content:	Gold 15.552 grams (0.500 troy ounces)
	Silver 0.509 grams (0.016 troy ounces)
	Copper 0.905 grams (0.029 troy ounces)

Quarter Ounce Gold Bullion Coin

Weight:	16.966 (0.5455 troy ounces)
Diameter:	22.00 millimeters (0.866 inches)

Thickness (est):   1.65 millimeters (0.065 inches)
Content: Gold 7.776 grams (0.250 troy ounces)
                        Silver 0.254 grams (0.008 troy ounces)
                        Copper 0.452 grams (0.015 troy ounces)

One Tenth Ounce Gold Bullion Coin

Weight: 3.393 grams (0.1091 troy ounces)
Diameter: 16.50 millimeters (0.650 inches)
Thickness (est):   1.27 millimeters (0.050 inches)
Content: Gold 3.110 grams (0.100 troy ounces)
                        Silver 0.102 grams (0.003 troy ounces)
                        Copper 0.181 grams (0.006 troy ounces)

The composition of all four gold bullion coins is a homogeneous alloy containing 91.67 percent gold, 3.0 percent silver and 5.33 percent copper.

One Ounce Silver Bullion Coin

Weight: 31.103 grams (1.000 troy ounces)
Diameter: 40.60 millimeters (1.598 inches)
Thickness (est):   3.04 millimeters (0.120 inches)
Content: Silver 31.072 grams (0.999 troy ounces)
                        Copper 0.031 grams (0.001 troy ounces)

The composition of the one ounce silver bullion coin is a homogeneous alloy containing a minimum of 99.9 percent silver and the balance copper.

Source: U.S. Dept. of Treasury, Bureau of the Mint.

Bibliography

Anderson, B.L. and P.L. Cottrell. *Money and Banking in England:* The Development of the Banking System, 1694–1914. London: David and Charles, 1974.

Bartlett, John. *Familiar Quotations.* Boston: Little, Brown, 1955.

Burns, A.R. *Money and Monetary Policy in Early Times.* New York: Sentry Books, 1965.

Du Bois, Cora. *People of Alor: A Social-Psychological Study of an East Asian Island.* Cambridge, Mass.: Harvard University Press, 1960.

Einzig, Paul. *Primitive Money in Its Ethnological, Historical and Economic Aspects.* Elmsford, N.Y.: Pergamon Press, 1966.

Farson, Negley. *Behind God's Back.* London: Victor Gollanez, 1940.

Galanoy, Terry. *Charge It: Inside the Credit Card Conspiracy.* New York: G.P. Putman's Sons, 1978.

Groseclose, Elgin Earl. *Money and Man: A Survey of Monetary Experiences.* Norman, Okla.: University of Oklahoma Press, 1972.

Hamilton, Alexander. *New Account of the East Indies.* William Foster, ed. New York: Da Capo. (Reprint of 1930 edition, Argorant Press.)

Henry, Lewis C. *Five Thousand Quotations for all Occasions.* New York: Garden City Books, 1952.

Hepburn, A. Burton. *History of Currency in the United States.* New York: Macmillan, 1924.

Homer, Sidney. *A History of Interest Rates.* New Brunswick, N.J.: Rutgers University Press, 1963.

Kemp, Arthur. *The Legal Quality of Money.* New York: Pageant Press, 1956.

Klise, Eugene S. *Money and Banking,* 5th ed. Cincinnati: Southwestern Publishing, 1972.

Lindheim, Leon. *Facts and Fiction About Coins.* Cleveland: World Publishing, 1968.

Mandell, Lewis. *Credit Card Use in the U.S.* Ann Arbor, Mich.: University of Michigan Press, 1972.

Mann, Fritz. *The Legal Aspect of Money.* Oxford, Eng.: Oxford at the Clarendon Press, 1953.

Massey, J. Earl. *America's Money: The Story of Our Currency and Coin.* New York: Thomas Y. Crowell, 1968.

McLoed, Tobert W. *Bank Credit Cards for EFTS.* Ann Arbor, Mich.: Research Press, 1977.

Reinfeld, Fred. *A Simplified Guide to Collecting American Paper Money.* Garden City, N.Y.: Hanover House, 1960.

Rist, Charles. *History of Monetary and Credit Theory (from John Law to Present Day).* New York: Macmillan, 1938.

Ritter, Lawrence S. and William L. Siber. *Money.* New York: Basic Books, 1970.

Rockoff, Hugh. *Drastic Measures: A History of Wage and Price Controls in the United States.* Cambridge, Eng.: Cambridge University Press, 1984.

Scott, Kenneth. *Counterfeiting in Colonial America.* Oxford, Eng.: Oxford University Press, 1957.

Sloan, Harold S. and Arnold J. Zurcher. *Dictionary of Economics.* New York: Barnes and Noble, 1970.

Sumner, William G. *A History of American Currency.* New York: Macmillan, 1924.

Taxay, Don. *The U.S. Mint and Coinage.* New York: Arco Publishing, 1966.

Timberlake, Richard H. *The Origins of Central Banking in the United States.* Cambridge, Mass.: Harvard University Press, 1978.

Wentworth, Harold and Stuart Berg Flexner. *The Pocket Dictionary of American Slang.* New York: Pocket Books, 1975.

Weston, Julian A. *The Cactus Eaters.* London: H.F.&G. Witherby, 1937.

Yeager, Leland B. *Proposals for Government Allocation of Credit.* Washington, D.C.: American Institute for Public Policy Research, 1977.

Yoeman, R.S. *A Guide Book of United States Coins,* 29th ed. Racine, Wisc.: Western Publishing, 1976.

————. "American Jurisprudence." Volume 34, U.S. Code, Title 18.

————. Annual Report of the Board of Governors of the Federal Reserve System, 1975.

————. "Back in the Money." Washington, D.C.: Federal Reserve Board, 1976.

————. "A Brief Summary of Coin and Currency." Federal Reserve Bank of New York, N.D.

————. "The Coin Situation: Review and Appraisal." Federal Reserve Bank of Dallas, October 1963.

————. "Counterfeiting." Department of the Treasury, United States Secret Service, 1972.

————. "Decline and Fall of the Gold Standard." Federal Reserve Bank of Dallas, January 1976.

————. "Evolution of Money and Banking in the United States." Federal Reserve Bank of Dallas, December 1975.

————. "Facts About United States Money." Department of the Treasury, Washington, D.C., December 1960.

————. "Fed Keeps Buried Cash." *San Antonio (Texas) Express,* February 26, 1976.

————. "The Federal Reserve System — Purposes and Functions." Board of Governors of the Federal Reserve System, Washington, D.C.

————. "Fundamental Facts About United States Money." Federal Reserve Bank of Atlanta, 1972.

————. "Fundamentals of Banking." New York: American Institute of Banking, 1945.

————. "Know Your Money." Department of the Treasury, United States Secret Service, 1972.

————. "The Monetary System of the United States." Board of Governors of the Federal Reserve System, February 1953.

————. "Money and Banking for High School Students." Austin, Texas: Texas Education Agency, 1956.

————. "A New Measure of the Money Supply." Federal Reserve Bank of St. Louis, July 1959.

————. *Standard 1976 U.S. Paper Money Catalogue.* New York: Scott, 1976.

————. "United States Treasury Bulletin No. 55." Department of the Treasury, 1971.

————. "You and the Law." The Readers Digest Association, Inc., 1971.

Index